Pilgrim's Promise

Getting Out of Egypt and Getting Egypt Out of Me

Bryan Cutshall

Pathway
P·R·E·S·S

Library of Congress Catalog Card Number: 98-65572

ISBN: 0871489872

DEDICATION

To my wife, *Faith*—my best friend and spiritual partner, who traveled with me through my own journey out of Egypt and into Canaan.

To *Brittany* and *Lindsay*, my finest earthly treasures who gave me my favorite title, Dad, and who fill my life with fun and joy. Your endless flow of creativity and energy give purpose and rhyme to my life.

To *Conway Jr.* and *Lois Wilson*, a teacher and tomato farmer who gave me my first scholarship and made it possible for me to go to college. Now I give you the gift of my first book. (I didn't forget!)

Table of Contents

FOREWORD

This is a book worth reading!

Bryan Cutshall is a successful young pastor who shows in this new book why the Old Testament can be such a powerful tool in coping with the problems of 21st-century living. He uses the path of the Hebrew children, getting out of Egypt, through the wilderness, and into the Promised Land, as a metaphor for life in modern times for all Christians, and he does it with clarity, simplicity, and great effectiveness.

In his book, Cutshall shows a love for the Old Testament and an understanding of it, and, even more importantly, an unusual ability to use Old Testament stories to illuminate and comment on contemporary issues. If read simply as a retelling of the Old Testament narrative of the flight from captivity, the book is worthwhile. It lifts the familiar account to the reader's attention in a fresh way.

But beyond the retelling of a familiar story is Cutshall's gift for making applications that are helpful to modern believers. Cutshall is not primarily an Old Testament theological scholar, but a pastor, and it shows. His pastoral eye for the application of principles is the strongest aspect of the book. In every chapter, he weaves the experiences of his pastoral ministry into the story of the Hebrew refugees, and with wonderful effect.

The pattern Cutshall follows is a simple one: getting out of Egypt, getting through the Wilderness, and getting into the Promised Land is the challenge everyone faces in every generation. There are memorable lessons in this book for every reader, whether a veteran traveler on the Christian path or a newcomer to it. I recommend it with enthusiasm.

Charles Paul Conn

Lee University

ACKNOWLEDGMENTS

Thank you, *Faith,* my loving wife, for encouraging me to believe in myself.

Thank you, *Brittany* and *Lindsay,* for telling me I am the best dad in the world, and that everyone would want to read my book.

Thanks to my parents, *Sammy* and *Rosemary Cutshall,* who introduced me to Jesus at an early age.

Thank you, *Eric* and *Sherry,* my brother and sister, for helping me "get into Egypt" (just kidding). You made the journey more interesting.

Thank you, *Lee University,* for requiring me to take Old Testament Survey and opening my eyes to this story for the first time.

Thank you, *Tammy Florence* and *Loretta Verde,* my secretaries, who proofread the manuscript many times.

Thanks to my *11 elders* who prayed for me each week while I was writing.

Thank you, *Twin Rivers,* my loving church family, who filled my life with love, joy, great illustrations, and many prayers.

Thank you, *Pat Bradbury,* my long-time friend, who encouraged me to read more and to write.

Thank you, *Wanda Griffith,* my editor, who patiently walked with me from Egypt to Canaan, one page at a time.

INTRODUCTION

Where are the champions—the present-day heroes of the Christian faith? Where are those who walk and talk what they claimed they would die for? Where are those who stand up to the naysayers and become yeah-sayers? It takes such little effort to be average, and almost no effort to be mediocre. Has the average, the status quo, become the accepted Christian norm of the day?

Victory is still possible for those who are willing to climb mountains, walk though threshing floors, and hold on to divine promises. Our goal is not to simply make it to heaven, or to barely stay out of hell. We have been promised quality of life—Canaan land! This promise is not a figment of hopeful imagination—it is a tangible reality for pilgrims who are willing to finish the journey and "come over." There are no shortcuts or quick-fix remedies. Ridding ourselves of carnality is a tough walk up the less-traveled road called "paying the price"—the only route to the winner's circle.

The Christian life is not merely existing until Christ comes back for His church. Rather, the Christian life is

- A battleground for not only fighting giants but also killing giants

- A pathway for not only walking through valleys but also walking out of valleys

- A place of trust where you not only live by faith but also live in faith

- A passageway of learning to focus your life, yoke with Christ, and align with the road map of God's Word

- A proclamation of a lifestyle of destiny and divine promise.

Leave the drudgeries behind; sound the trumpet of war to Satan's forces, declaring your determination to join the land of the living. Leave a legacy of victory behind for those who dare pursue the tracks of the determined. **Get up**, **get out**, and **get on** with a life filled with exploits of excellence.

With these convictions I write this book, which not only identifies the struggles within but also sheds light on the less-traveled trail leading to Canaan. Come join the pilgrimage of the Israelites. Identify with their struggles. Learn from their mistakes. Feast on their manna, and prepare for a new way of living . . . living on His promises.

PART I

EGYPT AND HOW TO GET OUT

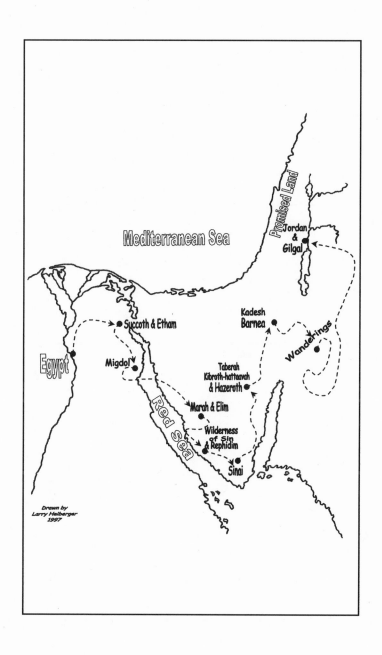

1

HOW DID EGYPT GET INTO ME?

Camping at Haran

Seeds of Greatness

"You keep flashing, making it hard for me to read your lips. Can you hold it for a minute?" she asked. "Let me know what *you* don't understand," she said to a puzzled reporter who strained to understand her answer.

The news conference was the first of many for the newly crowned Miss America who became deaf at the age of 11, two years after a reaction to a DPT shot. Heather Whitestone, a 21-year-old junior at Jacksonville State University, has only 5 percent hearing in her left ear. Heather reads lips, wears a large hearing aid, and uses sign language to compensate for her loss of hearing.

Her character reflects her philosophy. She views her disability, not as a handicap, but says, "The most handicapped person in the world is a *negative thinker*." She goes on to say her mother told her as a child that the last four letters of *American* spell *"I CAN."*

Heather traveled throughout the United States on a grueling speaking circuit declaring to young people (with and without disabilities) that "anything is possible!"

During the talent portion of the *Miss America Pageant*, Heather performed a ballet routine that brought the audience to tears as she danced to the music "Via Dolorosa." She did it by feeling the vibrations from the music, counting the beats in her head and synchronizing her dance movements to reflect changes in pitch.

What motivated Heather to accomplish such stunning achievements? Was it a special advantage or privilege that she had over others in life? Was it money, pedigree, or influence that brokered her success? Maybe it was extraordinary talent or intellect that did it. No, in spite of the handicaps, hardships, and heartbreaks, Heather achieved the impossible because of her belief that she could overcome any problem that threatened her from achieving her goals. Heather's formula for success is simple. Anyone who chooses to use it can attain high levels of accomplishment—even the impossible. Her formula is this:

1. Believe you are who God says you are.
2. Anything is possible.

Destined for Greatness

Deep in the soul of mankind are seeds of success

... seeds sown by God when He created mankind. This is why men and women compete against each other, craving to be on top, to win. The image of mankind's Maker reflects upon the soul and dreams for success and victory.

God is whole and complete. When man was created by God, he received the reflection (in measure) of God's nature. Humanity's prototype was made complete in every way, fitted to win.

Down but Not Out

When man fell, these precious seeds were exposed to Satan's spiritual fallout. The damage was total and complete. A hundred Hiroshimas or a thousand Nagasakis could not compare to the destructive force and damage sustained by the mind, soul, and body of mankind.

When Mount St. Helens belched forth fire and brimstone, tens of thousands of square miles of Eden-like landscape were suddenly transformed into a hellish moonscape unfit for habitation. Life was instantly extinguished. The crisp scent of springtime changed into the acrid stench of death and destruction that will last for years to come.

When Adam fell he was totally corrupted. The image of God, once aglow in man's heart, flickered. God's image in man's heart became vitiated.

So it is with fallen man. He reflects a distorted

image of his Creator. His values, goals, dreams, emotions, and physical well-being have all been affected. What once was a clear reflection of God's image is now marred and corrupted.

Man's fall(out) was far-reaching—more so than the debacle of the Chernobyl nuclear power station in Russia. When the protective superstructure was breached, it released billows of radioactive chemicals into the atmosphere, infecting thousands with sickness and death. This fallout does not discriminate. It takes its toll on men, women, and children.

Two Threads

A powerful analogy of how fallen creation influences and affects everything within it is found in the Old Testament Book of Genesis. Of the many types, historical accounts, revelations, and relationships given in this book, two threads run throughout its pages. One is the golden thread of achievement and freedom; the other is the black thread of failure and bondage.

The golden thread of achievement begins with the promises of God.

The Promise

Mankind started down the long spiral of disobedience, trapped forever in an endless cycle of failure. The forces of a fallen nature were pulling him farther and faster toward destruction. He repeated the same mistakes as he tried, without success, to break this cycle of misery and mediocrity.

Until one day God planted in the heart of man a noble seed of His promises that ultimately led man to Him. This journey of faith began as an excursion of trust, relying solely upon His promises as the road map. The pathway of promise, as it relates to Egypt, began with a pilgrim named Abram. We pick up his story and the beginning of his voyage in Genesis 12:1-4:

> The Lord had said to Abram, "Leave your country, your people and your father's household and go to the land I will show you. I will make you into a great nation and I will bless you; I will make your name great, and you will be a blessing. I will bless those who bless you, and whoever curses you I will curse; and all peoples on earth will be blessed through you." So Abram left, as the Lord had told him (*NIV*).

God selected Abram to break through the milieu of evil and debauchery sin had bred. Abram, probably much like anyone today, was not superman. His society was in turmoil, and everyone was doing his or her own thing.

Suddenly life as he knew it changed. God promised Abram amazing things during his lifetime — achievements that would impact the entire human race for all time. God himself guaranteed the fulfillment of these promises. God promised Abram:

1. He would father a great nation of people.

2. He would have God's blessing rest upon him and his descendants.

3. He would be a blessing to the nations of the world.

God planted in Abram's heart the seed of His promises. Now it became Abram's responsibility to obey. However, the "fallout" of a fallen nature affected Abram and, as we shall see, he constantly fought a battle against the pull of the world trying to reclaim him.

Abram was living at his father's house. His entire family worshiped Sin, the moon god. Before God could fulfill His divine plan in Abram's life, He had to get Abram away from Sin and get the influence of Sin out of Abram.

Haran—the Crossroads

Soon Abram was off with a band of travelers following the dream of a better life . . . a promise God told him would be fulfilled in a land called Canaan. This became Abram's destination. However, many delays and detours occurred because of the pull of family and friends.

Abram first traveled from his home, Ur of the Chaldeans, to Haran (which means "road"). He lived here with his family for five years. This was the first of many tests of faith Abram would encounter on his long journey. He must say goodbye to his past if he chose to go farther down the pathway of promise. Walking to the edge of the city each morning, he felt the pull of the horizon—a place flowing with milk and honey. But returning to the home of an aged father, he hid the promises in his heart to beat out the hours of another day.

Abram must have had these thoughts: *Do I see a new horizon? Or is it a spotlight keeping me in touch with reality? Where do I go from here?*

- Haran—a crossroads of choice between obedience and disobedience.

- Haran—family on one side, God on the other.

- Haran—wrestling between the flesh and the spirit.

- Haran—battlefields of dreams and realities.

- Haran—the land between old habits and hope.

That's Haran.

With each day Abram reminded himself that Canaan was waiting. The beckoning call of God tugged at his heart. Would this be the day to take the giant step of faith? Could he walk into his dying father's room and tell him he was leaving? Days turned into months and months to years. Before

Abram knew it, he had lived in Haran, the city of limbo, five years — five years filled with dreams and soul-searching.

After the death and burial of his father, Terah, Abram finally continued his pursuit of the promise. During this period of indecision, the blessings of God's promises were delayed, a consequence of saying yes too late. God is always faithful, but it seems that Abram forfeited his first season of blessings.

The Land of Promise

After traveling approximately 240 miles from Haran, Abram and his family came to Shechem, a city in Canaan (Genesis 12:4-6). The small caravan approached the city with elation. The fathers of Shechem were unaware of God's promise. The next morning Abram was led by the spirit to a high place where God affirmed the promise: "To your offspring I will give this land" (v. 7, *NIV*).

God was refining Abram's character in a pagan land infested with idolatry and wickedness. The great pastor Henry Ward Beecher said, "If a man cannot be a Christian in the place where he is, he cannot be a Christian anywhere." One could also say: If a man cannot be faithful where he is, he will not be faithful anywhere. Abram clung to the vision God had given him. In the midst of ridicule, rejection, and isolation, Abram built altars and worshiped God. His dream of fulfilling God's promises burned brightly in his heart . . . until famine hit. With starving herds and a lack of food, Abram's faith was stretched to the limit. Would he hold on?

Down to Egypt—the High Price of Disobedience

Rumors from traveling caravans said there was plenty to eat in Egypt. Instead of trusting God, Abram began thinking about leaving Canaan, taking the easy road and going "down to Egypt" (v. 10). Finally Abram announced to his family, "We are moving to Egypt to ride out the famine."

Egypt is a type of the world—a detour from God's promises. Abram's promise would never materialize in Egypt. His dreams and goals would die a slow death on the road of disobedience.

Abram's journey to Egypt was provoked by famine; however, he got into trouble with Pharaoh and was asked to leave the country. Later, Isaac was warned by God to stay out of Egypt (Genesis 26:2). But many years afterward, Jacob and his sons went to Egypt at the invitation of Joseph, who had been elevated to rulership (45:5-11). Again, God's people went to Egypt to avoid famine. After the famine and Joseph's death, however, they became slaves of Pharaoh. After 430 years of staying in Egypt, they were ready to leave.

The phrase "down to Egypt" is used 16 times in

the Bible, whereas Scripture refers to people going "up out of Egypt" 33 times. Disobedience always leads downward and away from God. God's plan for you and me is to live on higher ground—the rarefied air where eagles soar, nesting on mountain peaks. God's plan also includes waiting and patience. "But they that wait upon the Lord shall renew their strength; they shall mount up with wings as eagles" (Isaiah 40:31).

Disobedience is always a detour—a detour that withholds the promises of God in our lives. As a child I was greatly influenced by a minister with a unique preaching and singing style. After many years, I lost touch with him. A few years ago I heard the terrible news that this man was sent to prison for murder. After learning the details preceding this event, I realized that Egypt's call eventually enticed him. He left the ministry, his wife, and his ministerial calling to pursue the "things of this world" in Egypt. Recently a pastor friend of mine visited him in prison. He said to the pastor, "Tell everyone you know, 'It's not worth it!' Tell them, 'Sin will take you farther than you ever thought you could go.'"

The chase cost him dearly. His total losses are unknown, but one thing is sure: he lost the season of blessings and promises preserved for this time in his life. Someone has expressed it in these words: "Sin will always take you farther than you want to go. Sin will always keep you longer than you want to stay. Sin will always cost you more than you can afford to pay."

Going Down to Egypt
Personal Evaluation

Read each of the following statements and answer **True** or **False**. After answering, please take time to reflect on your answers to determine areas in your life that need prayer.

1. I truly believe that God has placed seeds of greatness in my life. _____

2. I am pursuing God's promises in my life. _____

3. I understand areas of weakness (temptations) that could potentially lure me into this world's system, and I am guarding against them. _____

4. I truly believe God has a plan for my life. _____

5. I truly believe God wants me to win and not to lose. _____

Meditate on the following questions and answer honestly.

1. Do I fully understand the high cost associated with disobeying God's plan for my life?

2. Am I waiting for something to happen before I follow God's plan for my life?

3. Am I fully aware that my disobedience will visit the generation that follows me unless I follow God's plan?

4. Do I really believe God wants me to live in victory?

5. Have I claimed the promises of God for my life?

Group Discussion

1. Abram is one of the greatest Old Testament patriarchs and is often considered a Bible hero. Discuss Abram, the ordinary man, and his struggles to take God at His word.

2. Name several promises of God and discuss how they apply to your current situation.

3. Ask a member of the group to share a personal experience of being at a crossroads.

4. Some people believe that the spiritual analogy of the Promised Land or Canaan is in reference to heaven. Explain.

5. Discuss why you think it is God's will for each person to be an overcomer.

6. List and discuss some of the seeds of greatness God has placed within each of us.

7. Discuss the last three sentences in chapter 1:

   • Sin will always take you farther than you want to go.

   • Sin will always keep you longer than you want to stay.

   • Sin will always cost you more than you can afford to pay.

Exercise

Arrange your chairs in a circle while each person in the group takes a turn standing in the middle. The other members of the group point out some seeds of greatness God has placed in that individual's life. The result will be positive and powerful as you see exhortation and encouragement personified.

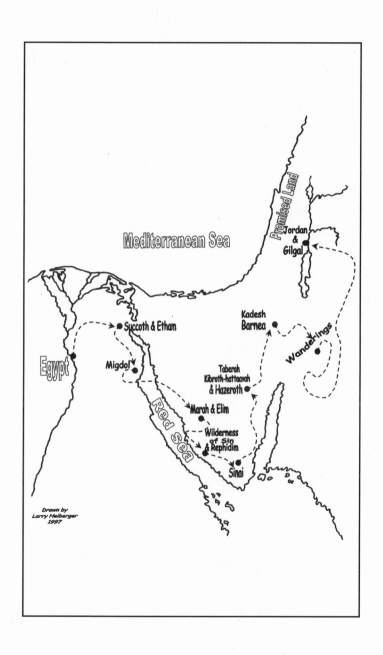

2

PASSING UNDER IN ORDER TO PASS OVER

The Story of the Passover

And on that very day the Lord brought the Israelites out of Egypt by their divisions.

The Lord said to Moses, "Consecrate to me every firstborn male. The first offspring of every womb among the Israelites belongs to me, whether man or animal." Then Moses said to the people, "Commemorate this day, the day you came out of Egypt, out of the land of slavery, because the Lord brought you out of it with a mighty hand. Eat nothing containing yeast. Today, in the month of Abib, you are leaving. When the Lord brings you into the land of the Canaanites, Hittites, Amorites, Hivites and Jebusites – the land he swore to your forefathers to give you, a land flowing with milk and honey – you are to observe this ceremony in this month" (Exodus 12:51 – 13:5, NIV).

From Famine to Familiarity

The Israelites went "down to Egypt" to escape famine, never intending to stay the length of time they actually did. They became comfortable in their new surroundings. Their families grew and prospered under Joseph's rulership. However, their comfort quickly ended when both Joseph and the Pharaoh who knew Joseph died. These descendants of Abraham became slaves of the new Pharaoh. They began to long and pray for their homeland. Egypt had become familiar and comfortable; now God had to awaken them in order to get them out of Egypt.

1. Familiarity is the thief of dreams. As each day takes the flavor of yesterday, the spinning wheel of life turns so steadily you forget to get off. Like a soaring buzzard with no place to land, the sameness of the world becomes like a drive across Kansas in the summer. Because each field and farm looks just like the ones passed for the last hundred miles, we stop looking. Soon the vision is gone. Hope and optimism leave with it, but we're not quite sure when.

Vision not only guides our future, but it also helps weed the present. Without vision we walk through life as a blind man with no guide — taking the same turns, making the same mistakes, re-creating the same old scenarios. Soon we can't even remember what life was like before.

2. Familiarity robs us of freshness that makes each day new and turns each laugh into a treasure.

3. Familiarity steals the music of life, tuning out the melodious words of family, friends, and God. In time even those closest to us begin to look like strangers. And the most distant person in our world is the man in the mirror. The "same old" face and phrases are nothing more than robotic.

4. Finally, familiarity blinds us to the dangers of complacency, placidity, and routine. Life is now painted with a coat of beige where all things blend. The things that were once considered threats to our future are common, and perhaps even comrades in this new world of the familiar.

Satan Had a Plot, but God Had a Plan

A once proud and blessed people became oppressed with the daily struggles of slavery. The horrifying sounds of whips cracking, people shouting, children carrying twigs for the fire and buckets of water for survival—all these comprised the long days and short nights of slavery. Separation from family members taxed the human spirit. But the promise that a redeemer would save them from this torturous life lived on. When? They didn't know.

His arrival was a shock to all. How could Moses, the adopted son of the princess, the one who killed the guard, a fugitive with a price on his head, be their deliverer? But God didn't, and still doesn't, consult the past to determine the future for those He calls. God used a series of plagues to soften the hearts of the Egyptians and to establish Moses as God's deliverer in the eyes of the Israelites.

God has an exit door for every person who ends up in Egypt. Whether He chooses to use a fugitive like Moses, a lionhearted shepherd like David, or a rough outdoorsman like John the Baptist, He has a plan! God always uses the ordinary to do the extraordinary. His plan today may not include 10 plagues and the "angel of death," but He has a way of delivering anyone willing to leave the land of mediocrity and despair.

Can God Get Me Out?

Headlines declared, "Plane Shot Down—Pilot Lost." Fear swept the nation as we learned of 29-year-old Captain Scott O'Grady, who was lost in the Bosnian jungle. Surviving on insects and wild plants, he cautiously waited for the trained and scrupulous rescue team who blasted in and out in two minutes.

Many others who are rescued daily from a life of imprisonment never make headlines. Missionary Dean Galyen, in his journeys through Africa, tells the story of a lady in Rwanda who was forced to kill her neighbor and her neighbor's three children. She asked, "Can your God save someone like me?" The answer is unequivocally, YES!

War has a way of corrupting and twisting the minds of the innocent. On one of my annual trips into the Central American country of El Salvador, I encountered a young man whom I will call Carlos. He too survived on insects and plants, fighting for the national army in their heinous civil war. He related stories of how he chopped men's heads off and sewed them up inside their bellies for a political demonstration. He tearfully poured out his soul relating how he murdered men while they were pleading and begging for their lives. His weary eyes disclosed volumes of untold stories, exposing windows to the chained and tormented mental wars of his soul. He too asked the question, "Can your God save a man like me?"

The answer was, and still is, "Yes." With the help of a Spanish interpreter, Carlos knelt in a room filled with American construction workers and said the sinner's prayer. Today he lives for God.

John was a drug user and a thief. He dropped out of school, had two children out of wedlock, and was in and out of every juvenile court in the city. He had no religious background. His language was profane; his appearance was back-alley street attire. Society had given up on John and stereotyped him as a psychotic sociopath. When I met him, only one person believed in him. That one person came out of Egypt, but went back in for John. She is a real heroine. She walked the aisle with John twice —

41

once to meet Jesus, and the other in matrimony. Today John is a healthy, productive Christian. He is a father, a hard worker, and a loving husband — free from the fears of tomorrow. He, too, got out.

Ordinary People, Ordinary Things

Heroes seldom look like heroes. Look at these attributes: simple, stuttering, scared, scorched, self-less, and sore. Does this sound like a hero to you? Yet Moses was the deliverer of the Israelites.

One of the greatest soulwinners I know is just a simple man. I have never seen him in a suit. His speech is common and simple. He began his own ministry called the "Stranded Motorist Ministry." While going to and from his work as a prison guard, he stops to help motorists who are stranded. While making adjustments and minor repairs, he tells the good news of the gospel and gives them a sermon on cassette tape. Through his ministry, people have been healed, saved, and delivered because some-one pointed the way "out of Egypt." It's a simple message and method, proclaimed by a simple man.

Although Moses was used mightily of God, the best thing he did was just hold up the exit sign. God has a road sign for every weary traveler. The mes-sage is always the same: "Turn right and keep going straight." Egypt gets confusing and complicated with its many roads and multiple choices. It's easy to get lost in Egypt, but the way out is still simple.

Through the Blood and Ready to Go

Moses declared to the Israelites, "The only way out of Egypt is through the blood" (see Exodus 12:1-23). Each household had to select an unblemished male lamb in its first year, take a sprig of hyssop and smear the blood upon the doorpost. Then they were to sit down and eat the meat with unleavened bread and bitter herbs. While eating, the family had to be ready to leave at any time. After dressing and arraying their doorpost with blood, the Israelites ate the Passover lamb, gathered the family together, and remained in their clothes and shoes (see v. 11). They did not know when their deliverer would call, so they had to be ready.

The moon hung low in a reddish wake. The king's palace was silent with the exception of chatter among the guards. Then God unzipped the veil, separating the temporary from the eternal, enough for the "angel of death" to step through. Silence hovered over the land as sleeping babes and grown men — the firstborn of each household — died in their sleep. As daylight broke, cries and screams could be heard from house to house. Women ran into the streets with dead babies, cursing the God of the Israelites. They also cursed the king for allowing this plague to come upon them.

That same morning Moses and Aaron were awakened, not by an angel, but rather by an angry guard who dragged them to the king's chambers.

The angry king, holding his dead son in his arms, ordered them to leave. The curses of the distraught queen mother could be heard as they hurried to the slave city of Goshen.

When the Israelites heard the prearranged signal, they scurried to the floor, harnessed their oxen, and lined their carts in a row. At last it was time to get out of Egypt (see vv. 29-33).

As the Israelites walked down Main Street in Egypt, they felt what every sinner feels walking toward the altar. They walked past the head slave master who was powerless to stop them. The Egyptians willingly gave the jewelry from their bodies to the Hebrew slaves as they marched out. Imagine a slave taking the signet ring (the signature of power) right off the hand of the head slave master. Perhaps Moses even said, "Stop! Get one last look at Egypt and never forget what life in slavery is like." They did not know the magnitude of this last look and how that image would serve as a guide for them to keep pressing on.

Next came the real test: Now that they were out of Egypt, could they ever get Egypt out of them? Part of experiencing freedom is the joy and thankfulness that come from remembering where God brought you from. Where were you when He found you?

Getting Out of Egypt

The plight of sin is bondage, and it is not

something we can escape by ourselves. It requires a deliverer. God has raised up many servants to point the way, but the ultimate deliverer is Jesus.

Egypt is always waiting with its enticements and charms. But so is Canaan. Egypt and Canaan co-exist in our world today. Egypt, a secular society with its system of selfishness, still enslaves. Many are chained to hopelessness and despair. Their lives are beaten down by the taskmasters of societal expectations and peer pressures. The taskmaster exists in many forms:

- The taskmaster of business robs us of time needed for personal growth and relationship development.

- The taskmaster of fear robs us of opportunities and personal achievement.

- The taskmaster of low self-esteem robs us of our self-worth.

- The taskmaster of the past robs us of our future.

- The taskmaster of anger robs us of joy.

- The taskmaster of jealousy robs us of security.

Many are still enslaved. The real Pharaoh is no longer on the throne, but the spirit of antichrist rules in his stead, dictating degrading morals and unethical codes. The king is still wicked and people are still in bondage.

In the midst of this confusion and gloom, a light shines through with the promise that will lead you to Canaan . . .

- The land of ownership
- The land of victory and fruitfulness
- The land where the deliverer, Jesus Christ, is king
- A place where giants fall and walls crumble.

Canaan is not free of challenge or peril, yet it stands as a symbol of victory where you can win over trouble and despair. In Canaan you find a land for overcomers, a land of rejoicing and praise. In Canaan, God goes before you into battle. He is your banner, your rock, your fortress, your buckler, your high tower—a place the righteous run to for safety.

You do not have to be a slave to sin any longer. Get up and get out of Egypt. The plan is still the same: There is a doorway covered with the blood of the Lamb. Walk through that door and follow Him to the Land of Promise. God designed you to be a winner. You weren't created for Egypt, you were created for Canaan. You weren't created to be a slave, you were created to be a conqueror. Come on . . . let's go to Canaan.

Getting Sin Out of Me
Personal Evaluation

Read each of the following statements and answer **True** or **False**. Please fill in the blanks after each question to use as a guideline for planning your route to victorious living.

1. I have allowed some of the important people in my life to become too familiar, thus not appreciating them for their value to me. ____ People I should appreciate more include _____

   _____.

2. There are things in my life I have tolerated that I know I should change. ____ The first thing I need to change is_____.

3. I know that I am saved because I have prayed the sinner's prayer. ____ The approximate anniversary of my salvation is____/____19____.

4. I haven't forgotten where God has brought me from. ____ I will not forget to thank God for bringing me out of _____.

5. I am comfortable around things I know are sinful. ____ I do not wish to participate in any sin; I will be more cautious of these temptations:

   _____.

47

Meditate on the following questions and answer honestly.

1. Do I fully realize not only what God saved me from, but also what He saved me from becoming?

2. Does sin make me uncomfortable, or is it familiar to me?

3. Do I consider myself a Christian, or am I in the process of becoming a Christian?

Group Discussion

1. The first sentence of chapter 2 contains the words "The Israelites went 'down to Egypt' . . . never intending to stay." Discuss the dangers of dabbling in sin.

2. Discuss the following symbols mentioned in the Exodus story and what they represent in New Testament salvation: Moses the deliverer, King Pharaoh, the spotless lamb, the blood of the lamb, the blood on the doorposts, the unleavened bread, the bitter herbs, the passing over of the "death angel," and the exodus from Egypt.

3. Discuss the benefit of remembering where God has brought you from.

4. Discuss the danger of forgetting where God has brought you from.

5. Moses was a simple and humble man whom God used to be the Old Testament *type of Christ*. Name modern-day ordinary men who could be classified as heroes of the faith.

6. Have someone in the group tell the story of his/her salvation experience.

7. Have someone in the group lead in the sinner's prayer.

Exercise

Do a *role play* of explaining the plan of salvation to someone who has never heard the gospel message.

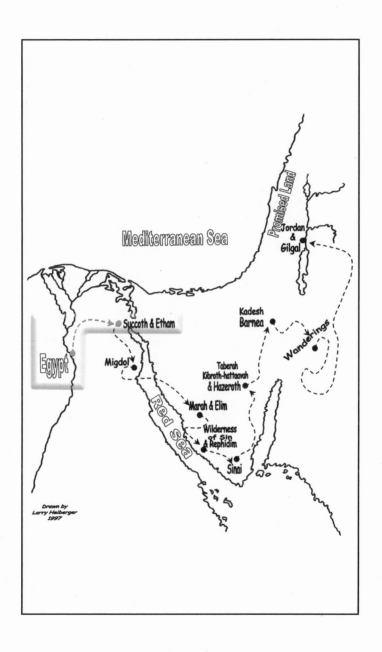

Mediterranean Sea

Promised Land

Jordan & Gilgal

Egypt

Succoth & Etham

Migdol

Red Sea

Kadesh Barnea

Wanderings

Taberah Kibroth-hattaavah & Hazeroth

Marah & Elim

Wilderness of Sin & Rephidim

Sinai

Drawn by
Larry Heiberger
1997

3

GOING THROUGH THE VALLEY
TO GET DELIVERANCE

Camping at the Valley of Succoth and Etham

*And it came to pass, when Pharaoh had let the people go, that **God led them not** through the way of the land of the Philistines, although that was near; for God said, Lest peradventure the people repent when they see war, and they return to Egypt: But **God led the people about, through the way of the wilderness of the Red sea**: and the children of Israel went up harnessed out of the land of Egypt* (Exodus 13:17, 18).

"Follow Me"

Do the following statements sound like empty phrases or incredible faith?

- "Here am I, send me" (Isaiah 6:8).
- "Where He leads me, I will follow" (E.W. Blandly).

- "I am Thine, O Lord, I have heard Thy voice" (Fanny J. Crosby).

- "I have decided to follow Jesus, no turning back, no turning back" (Traditional).

The intent of each of God's children is to follow Him unconditionally; that is, even when adversities come. It is then we learn the difference between God's point of view and man's. God sees the overall picture from beginning to end. We try to see; we strain our reasoning trying to understand, but at best we can see only the present which is merely a glimpse of the big picture. "Follow Me" was the initial instruction Jesus gave His disciples in the early ministry years. "Follow Me" was the implied instruction given to Abraham, Moses, and Joshua. Sometimes the only instruction we get from the Lord is "Follow Me."

Jesus said, "Follow me, and *I will make* you fishers of men" (Matthew 4:19). No more details, just "follow Me," He says. Jesus wanted to make disciples of all who would follow Him. God said to Moses in essence, "Follow Me, and I will turn the heart of Pharaoh. I will draw him to a place I have prepared for him and his army." Faith is difficult only when we leave God and His promises out of the equation.

Is This the Right Way, God?

Canaan . . . only 18 days from Egypt. Many had

made the journey before. Everyone knew the way, it seemed—except God. He did not lead them on the simple 18-day route. Instead, He told Moses to head this fearful caravan into the wilderness. They didn't have to go. They could have remained in Egypt, but they went with the faith that God feeds where He leads. God knows where you are headed, and He knows where He must take you to get you there. God's leadership is long-term. He is not interested in our shortcut systems. God is trying to mold our character. He is more interested in the finished product than in the comfort of a single day. That's why He said, "All things work *together for good* to them that love God, to them who are the called according to his purpose" (Romans 8:28). This is not suggesting that all things that work together are necessarily good. Like a giant jigsaw puzzle, the portrait of who we are is formed in His divine plan for our lives. Each circumstance we encounter may not seem to have a significant purpose, but when God writes the final chapter, He will pull it all together in two words: "Well done!"

His Ways Are Above Our Ways

Many years ago while sitting in a missions service, I was challenged to go into the country of El Salvador in Central America. The urge to go was more overwhelming to me than the uncertainty. El Salvador was in the heat of a brutal civil war, making it difficult for missionaries to enter. I made my plans

●

to go and found six brave souls to accompany me. Two weeks before our departure, I received word that the guerrilla forces had sent a ransom notice to the man who would serve as my contact. They were demanding $20,000 (U.S. currency) in exchange for letting him live. After being notified, the members of my team all felt the situation was too risky, so they backed out. I, too, was tempted to stay, but the call kept ringing in my ears to go. Many advised me to cancel my plans, but I knew in my heart that I was supposed to go.

The day came for me to fly into El Salvador alone. I really didn't know what to expect. I was abruptly greeted by a brusque group of soldiers. They frisked me, disassembled my camera, and poked me with their guns while going through my luggage. There were many days during my stay when I questioned the Lord about my presence there. Each evening I was locked behind six iron doors in a room with no ventilation. We had to disinfect and debug the room each evening, which meant going to sleep breathing insecticide. I would lie awake sweating, listening to gunfire, screams, and planes flying overhead. I visited churches that had been bombed and spoke with pastors whose family members had been killed.

When the trip was over, I was exhausted, dehydrated, and hospitalized. I was glad I went, but really had no definite plans to return. Approximately one year later I heard the same voice drawing me again. I fought the feeling for many months. Finally, I said yes to God and began to make plans for my second trip into the country.

By this time the country had signed a peace treaty with the opposing forces. Once again I made an appeal for short-term missionaries. This time, to my amazement, 32 people signed up to go, and we built a church building in only eight days. We were the first American team from our denomination to build a church in El Salvador. Since then, we have gone back every year to build another church.

God wasn't calling me to make a fearful, onetime visit. He was wanting me to open the door so hundreds of short-term missionaries could go into the country and build up His kingdom.

Detours

"And it came to pass, when Pharaoh had let the people go, that God led them not through the way of the land of the Philistines, although that was near; for God said, Lest peradventure the people repent when they see war, and they return to Egypt " (Exodus 13:17).

Premature blessings . . . do such things exist? In our world of "instant everything," we sometimes forget that quality takes time. The people of Israel simply were not ready to handle the challenges of Canaan. This was the purpose for this boot camp in the desert. No one was being punished — just trained.

Can you imagine how life would turn out if God answered every prayer the way we asked Him to? God would not be in control anymore — we would. He would be our Genie in a bottle, catering to our every whim and desire. There would be no dependence, no trust, no faith, no growth, no personal development, no transformation, no molding or reshaping, no character. God would be in the hands of man, not man in the hands of God.

God told the Israelites, "I will not drive them [the people of Canaan] out from before thee in one year; lest the land become desolate, and the beast of the field multiply against thee. By little and little I will drive them out from before thee, until thou be increased, and inherit the land" (Exodus 23:29, 30).

Little by little — that is how success is achieved. Not one big win, but many small wins compounded. Dr. Mike Murdock said, "The secret to success is found in our daily routine." God knows this and is trying to teach us to win little by little.

If God delays us, it is only to get our eyes off ourselves and back on Him and His promise. Satan, however, detours us to keep us from reaching our goals. He sidetracks us with selfish interests so that we lose our way.

Detours — things that deter your focus and defer your interest — will change your entire course or direction. Delays are only learning experiences to help you focus more aptly on the journey. The difference between a detour and a delay is simple: When direction takes you away from your desired goal, it's a *detour*; if it complements and corresponds with your original destination, then it is simply a *delay*.

He Leads Me to and Through the Valley

There are plenty of mountains in God's kingdom, just as there are plenty of grassy meadows, rippling brooks, and valleys. Why valleys? God led the Israelites to camp at the Valley of Succoth, just before the Red Sea. Psalm 23 gives fresh insight about valleys:

> The Lord is my shepherd; I shall not want. He maketh me to lie down in green pastures: he leadeth me beside the still waters. He restoreth my soul: he leadeth me in the paths of righteousness for his name's sake. Yea, though I walk through the valley of the shadow of death, I will fear no evil: for thou art with me; thy rod and thy staff they comfort me. Thou preparest a table before me in the presence of mine enemies: thou anointest my head with oil; my cup runneth over. Surely goodness and mercy shall follow me

59

all the days of my life: and I will dwell in the house of the Lord for ever.

Notice that *He leads me beside still waters*. This is the way of peace. Here He restores my soul. Also, *He leads me in paths of righteousness* — not highways, not sidewalks, not even trails, but paths. A worn-down place where few have trod . . . places few have seen . . . fruit that few have tasted . . . scenes few have revered.

Then *He leads me to the valley*. And if He leads you *to* the valley, He'll take you *through* the valley. In the valley I find . . .

- A place to remember
- A place to stop
- A place to be still and know God
- A place to meet Him.

The valley is the place where we are restored and refreshed for the journey ahead.

The valley of Succoth had a distinct purpose. In the valley God's people heard Him speak. He lives there because He is the lily of the valley. In the valley we remember where God has brought us from — sin, bondage, slavery. When we remember what God delivered us from, we will declare not only what He saved us from but also what He saved us from becoming. We may not be what we want to be, but thank God we're not *what we used to be* and we are not *what we could have been.*

Next Stop—Etham

> And they took their journey from Succoth,
> and encamped in Etham, in the edge of the
> wilderness. And the Lord went before them
> by day in a pillar of a cloud, to lead them the
> way; and by night in a pillar of fire, to give
> them light; to go by day and night: He took
> not away the pillar of the cloud by day, nor
> the pillar of fire by night, from before the
> people (Exodus 13:20-22).

Etham is where God made Himself visible to the
nation of Israel. The scene was a frightening and
august sight. The wind increased in velocity like a
racer revving the engines for a race. The sun became darkened as the air became thin. Clouds
rolled in huge billows as if they were boiling from
a furnace. The ground shook, not like an earth-
quake, but with a steady quiver. The trees and rocks
stood like soldiers in uniform. This was a most
unusual and fearful sight.

Suddenly a Shekinah cloud began to spiral from
the heavens to the place where the Hebrews
camped. As it touched the ground, an invisible
mold appeared in the shape of a huge column. Once
formed, it stood majestically . . . a pillar made of
clouds. This Shekinah was so bright and fluores-
cent it was hard to look upon. It glowed as though

a fire were burning in its belly. The nation knew God was in their midst.

This indescribable image of God was displayed in two significant forms — a *pillar of cloud* and a *pillar of fire*. The Hebrew word for pillar is *ammuwd,* which means "a standing column." The purpose of a pillar is to *hold something up*. Suddenly in the desert they discovered that the burden of this journey was not all up to them.

Faith Holds Up the Man Who Holds Up the Faith

There is a song which says in essence that we do not know our future, but we do know who holds our future. What stupendous truth lies in this profound phrase.

Elder David and Mary Haynes had their faith put to the test. They raised a beautiful family and instilled in them the truths of God. Their middle daughter, Leatha, married Pastor Rick Whitter. The Hayneses now had two beautiful granddaughters. When their youngest granddaughter was only 3, she was diagnosed with a rare type of cancer called neuroblastoma.

Elder David and Mary decided to stay with Pastor Rick and enter into a time of spiritual warfare. Daily he walked the floor of a 12-by-14 room, praying hour upon hour. However, each evening when he returned home, he noticed her condition continued to worsen. He intensified the prayer time and coupled it with fasting. The four entered into intense personal "war-prayer." Convinced that God would not let them down, they prayed fervently to the point of exhaustion.

This battle continued for 90 days. Two days after her 4th birthday, as they sat in their home in Florida, they watched the life slowly leave their little granddaughter. Elder Haynes, the man of faith, as I call him, picked up his Bible and for a moment was tempted to throw it out, but instead he clung to it. The months passed, the pain diminished, but the question lingered. Satan thought he had finally detoured David and Mary Haynes.

A few months later in a church service, Elder Haynes was asked to pray for those who had come forward. As I handed the microphone to him, I saw his countenance change. All at once the most powerful prayer I have ever heard burst from his lips. The more he prayed, the more powerful it became. Each person who came up for prayer that morning was delivered. I watched as one of the greatest prayer warriors was birthed through an adverse incident.

Since then he has made missionary trips where God has performed miracles through his prayers. One day while on a work site in a foreign country, he prayed in agreement with another brother and saw three distinct miracles in one afternoon.

In 1994, while in El Salvador, Elder Haynes prayed for God's intervention because the only water source we had was being rationed. That evening, without a cloud in sight, it rained enough to fill every water barrel and basin. National Overseer David Peraza, a native El Salvadorian, told us it was the first time in his life he had ever seen it rain in late February (three months after the rainy season is over).

Faith holds up the man who holds up the faith!

Getting Out of the Valley

Personal Evaluation

Read each of the following statements and answer **True** or **False.**

1. I truly believe I am following God as He leads me on a spiritual journey. _____

2. I have complete faith that God is in control of my life. _____

3. I can accept a "no" answer from God. _____

4. I can sense God's presence in the valleys of my life. _____

5. I am determined to keep the faith, no matter what. _____

Meditate on the following questions and answer honestly.

1. Do I truly know how to follow God as He leads the way?

2. Can I accept the fact that a premature blessing could do more harm to me than good and that I should trust God to bless me as I mature in Him?

3. Do I view each valley as a learning experience or as a delay in my spiritual walk?

4. Even though I may never see a pillar of fire or a Shekinah cloud, do I still see God in other forms? How do I see God?

5. Do I trust God even when it is inconvenient?

Group Discussion

1. Discuss how we can know the difference between God's leading and following after our own plans.

2. Discuss the danger of a premature blessing.

3. Have a member of the group share a personal experience of a lesson learned in the valley.

4. Discuss Exodus 23:29, 30: "I will not drive them out from before thee in one year; lest the land become desolate, and the beast of the field multiply against thee. By little and little I will drive them out from before thee, until thou be increased, and inherit the land."

5. The "pillar of fire" image of God is important because it signifies that God is the column that is holding up the spiritual building. How can we relate to that image in our day? Is God still a pillar of fire in the desert?

6. Discuss the difference between a test of faith and a temptation.

7. Discuss what our Christian character would be
    like if we never had a valley or a testing of our
    faith. How long would it take before we became
    spoiled children who pitched tantrums to get
    God's attention?

Exercise

Have each member of the group write a letter to
a discouraged friend who is presently in the valley.
If the friend responds, ask his or her permission to
read the response letter to the group. Everyone will
be able to share in the ministry of encouragement,
as well as the victory of overcoming.

67

PART II

THE WILDERNESS AND HOW TO GET THROUGH

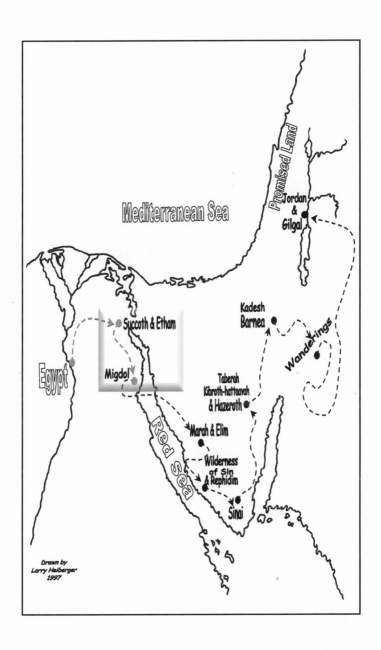

4

GETTING RID OF THE PAST

Camping at Migdol and the Red Sea

And he made ready his chariot, and took his people with him: And he took six hundred chosen chariots, and all the chariots of Egypt, and captains over every one of them. And the Lord hardened the heart of Pharaoh king of Egypt, and he pursued after the children of Israel: and the children of Israel went out with an high hand. But the Egyptians pursued after them, all the horses and chariots of Pharaoh, and his horsemen, and his army, and overtook them encamping by the sea, beside Pi-hahiroth, before Baal-zephon. And when Pharaoh drew nigh, the children of Israel lifted up their eyes, and, behold, the Egyptians marched after them; and they were sore afraid: and the children of Israel cried out unto the Lord (Exodus 14:6-10).

The Past

The door opens. The light is dim. Everything is covered in last year's dust, including faddish-style clothes that now look silly. The handmade sentimentalities are barely recognizable. There is your diary and an old toy, but you still haven't found what you're looking for.

Plundering through the old newspapers and worn-out shoes, you finally see the corner of it underneath an empty candy box you thought might come in handy one day. At last, the old shoe box filled with photos is recovered. These photos captured those silly hairdos, toothless children, embittered frowns, and playful smiles. This is the past.

Some photos bring back joyful memories; others . . . well, you just wish someone would throw them away. Here's one that makes you laugh. That one brings a tear. And suddenly you find one you forgot was there. The pain starts all over again. How can a photo bring on such a flood of emotions? There you are with a wadded-up photo in your hand and a hidden file reopens in your mind. It's the past filled with mistakes, failures, trouble, pain, hurts, and disappointments — all part of an old mental file sealed years ago. Here it surfaces again. Wouldn't it be nice to bury it once and for all?

Israel's Past

Can you imagine what hundreds of years of slavery can do to a culture? Many generations had endured the hardships of the whipping post, a slave's portion of food, a straw bed, and perhaps a chance that they couldn't even choose their own wives. And females were valued only for their ability to bear more children. It was a prison way of thinking. No wonder God couldn't give them Canaan. He could take them out of the slave master's reach, but they still had the mentality of slaves, not conquerors.

Could Caleb say, "Give me this mountain" at this point? (see Joshua 14:12). Could young Joshua say, "As for me and my house, we will serve the Lord"? (see 24:15). Their fathers, grandfathers, and great-grandfathers were slaves before them. This was the only way of life they knew. Their potential lay dormant, exposed to only one way of thinking— they had to get out.

Getting out was the first step to discovering the champion inside. But what about the slave masters? Would God's people always be looking over their shoulders to see if these abusers would creep up on them again?

Living Life in the Rearview Mirror

Too many of God's children live defeated lives because they allow the past to hover over their heads like dark clouds of fear. Even when doors to the future open, they remain chained to the past. They walk as through a minefield, never knowing which step will blow their cover and expose their past. This heinous monster visits them in their sleep. On the outside they are smiling, but on the inside scenes from the past are on continuous play. If only someone could turn it off, make it go away.

A young lady whom I will call Jackie came to my office crying, heaving up years of emotional pain, guilt, and abuse. Most of her problems stemmed from severe abuse during adolescence. During our sessions I asked her to complete an exercise. With her eyes closed and thoughts cleared, she began to detail a normal day in her life at the age of 10. This sensitive exercise touched the heart of her pain and fear. In the same manner, I asked her to detail the activities of her day on that present day. Things had changed. Her day began at 6 a.m. with children to feed, a husband's lunch to make, clothes to wash, a house to clean, and an appointment to keep with me. I followed the exercise with this question: "What is the difference?" She said, "Things have changed. I have changed."

The magic of that moment was instrumental in freeing her from her painful past. She was a grown woman who still lived with fears of the past. We must be free from the past in order to live in the present.

The Devil in My Rearview Mirror

Satan wants to haunt us with our past through the mechanism of worry. He uses it as a weapon of intimidation, twisting the facts, causing us to worry about incidentals that are magnified out of proportion. He uses our God-given gift of imagination, coupled with Hollywood images, to create very unrealistic scenarios. This is why the Word of God instructs us to use the weapons of our warfare against Satan by casting down those imaginations (2 Corinthians 10:4, 5). Carman, the contemporary Christian artist, states, "When the devil reminds you of your past, simply remind him of his future."

Another way Satan uses our past against us is by reminding us of our failures in life. Failure is a part of life everyone experiences. When God forgives us of failure, we must forgive ourselves so that Satan cannot use it as ammunition against us.

Rahab was a prostitute in Jericho. Her family was the only family spared in the Jericho conquest. She married an Israelite and became an ancestor of Jesus. She is mentioned in the Matthew account of the genealogy of Christ (1:5).

Many of God's "mighty men of valor" had failures in their past. At one time . . .

- Abraham lied.
- Isaac lied.
- Jacob lied and deceived.
- Moses murdered.
- David murdered and committed adultery.
- Solomon allowed idolatry.

- Elijah doubted.
- Peter denied Christ.
- Paul killed Christians.

God doesn't consult your past to determine your future.

The Camp of Migdol and the Red Sea

Migdol represents a place of fear and helplessness. The sea is in front of you. The enemy is behind you, and mountains are on both sides of you. You are boxed in. You feel like a grape going through the winepress, crushed under the pressure. Stress builds up. Hopelessness settles in. Anxieties mount. Anger is building. This is Migdol — a place where Israel confronted her past. God told Moses to have the people do three things:

1. Stand still!
2. See God!
3. Hold your peace!

Stand still. The enemy is approaching . . . stand still. You can taste the dust from the fast-moving chariots . . . stand still. The sounds of hooves are beating in your ears . . . stand still. One cries out, "There is no place to run"; Moses cries out, "Stand still!" Mothers clinch their children close to them. Fathers pick up a garden tool or a shepherd's staff as their only means of defense.

Moses is now yelling, "Stand still." The cattle are scurrying restlessly. The approaching horde is shaking the ground. The 15-mile stretch of sea is too far to swim. The mountains are too steep to climb. Families stand clannishly close as if they are in shock.

Sometimes in our lives the only direction we get from the Lord is to stop and stand still. We view life with a new perspective when we stop. I once tried to videotape my wife's hometown from a moving vehicle. The footage came out blurred and meaningless. Our lives also get out of focus when we forget to stop. It is easy to think that the cure for every battle is to do something. Sometimes the only orders we get from God are to do nothing. Doing nothing does not mean that we go into denial. It does not mean we do not have responsibilities. Sometimes God wants us to stop long enough to regain our focus. In the chaos of confusion, stopping settles the dust and allows us time to revisit our original motives and intentions. Stopping helps us see what God is doing.

See God. God is everywhere, but we have to look for Him. Those who seek will find God in every circumstance of life. You can't see God until you are still.

In 1995 I had enlarged nodules on my vocal cords and was advised to have them surgically removed. The surgery involved having my vocal cords stripped so that new skin could grow back. The clincher for me was the waiting period. I could not speak a word for three weeks. The next weeks I could only whisper. For a minister who preaches five to seven times a week to be told he could not say a word for one whole month was bad news!

I went in for surgery and began my month of silence. During that month I discovered a whole new world I never knew existed. My 70-hour work week had kept me too busy talking to stop and listen. I was too busy asking God to make my dreams come true to see His dreams for my life. Amazingly, I began to see things God's way. In the quietness I could meditate on His goodness and allow Him to open my spiritual eyes so that I could see with His vision.

Many years ago American astronauts and Russian cosmonauts went into space to find God. One group's conclusion was this: "We looked everywhere and we did not see any sign of God." The other group's conclusion was this: "Everywhere we looked we saw God. The universe was filled with signs of His presence."

Hold your peace. Imagine that! The enemy was storming and God wanted the Israelites to hold their peace. Isn't peace the feeling we get at the end of the day when we prop our feet up and sip a cup of gourmet coffee? Or perhaps it is the feeling of getting the children in bed and then soaking in a bubble bath.

No, that isn't peace; that is only relaxation. God wasn't asking them to recline. He wasn't asking them to ignore the approaching army. He was asking them not to give up in defeat.

Two artists were asked to paint a picture depicting peace. One great artist painted an 8-year-old boy sitting in a fishing boat on a perfectly calm lake. It symbolized peace as the absence of problems.

The other artist painted a gigantic waterfall whose ferocious and threatening waters avalanched off the side of a steep cliff. Hanging over the cliff was the branch of a tree with a bird's nest filled with eggs. The spray of the water rose just a few feet from the nest. This symbolized peace as reliance on something greater than ourselves (in this case, the tree) in the midst of the threat.

I agree with the second artist.

- Peace is not found on a calm lake; it is seeing the Master walking on the water in the middle of the storm.

- Peace is not staying home and tending sheep; it is walking into the battlefield with a sling shot in one hand, a stone in the other, and God in your sights.

- Peace is not sitting at the King's right hand; it is walking in the furnace with the Fourth Man.

Peace cannot come without peril. God said, "I

will keep him in perfect peace whose mind is stayed on Me" (see Isaiah 26:3). The following poem was written for my dear friend Jerry O'Bryan, whose spirit is strong though his body is in a battle with Crohn's disease.

THE COST OF CHARACTER

There is no mountain without a valley.

There is no solution without a problem.

There is no song without a sorrow.

There is no dream without discontent.

There is no strength without pain.

There is no courage without fear.

There is no victory without a battle.

There is no success without sacrifice.

There is no healing without a wound.

There is no miracle without a need.

There is no peace without a peril.

There is no character without the anvil and the hammer.

– Bryan Cutshall

God's Ambush

And the Lord said unto Moses, Wherefore criest thou unto me? speak unto the children of Israel, that they *go forward*: But lift thou up thy rod, and stretch out thine hand over

the sea, and divide it: and the children of Israel shall go on dry ground through the midst
of the sea. . . .

And Moses stretched out his hand over the
sea; and the Lord caused the sea to go back
by a strong east wind all that night, and made
the sea dry land, and the waters were divided. And the children of Israel went into
the midst of the sea upon the dry ground:
and the waters were a wall unto them on
their right hand, and on their left (Exodus
14:15, 16, 21, 22).

Storm clouds gathered as the voice of God began to sing the song of revenge. The seas trembled
and hid themselves. The foot of God was about to
step on the enemy of the Israelites. The desert
sky was blackened with the arrival of God's war
party. Lightning bolts hurtled like sparks from the
wheels of God's chariots as they approached the
battlefield. God stepped one foot into the sea and
cleared a path for Moses and His children. With
His hand, God nudged Pharaoh and his army toward the sea. They approached with caution and
terror. The storm overhead confused them. The
dry ground beneath their feet made no sense. God
gave one pull on the hook in Pharaoh's jaw and
he rode his horrified beast onto the sea's floor.
This was Pharaoh's appointment with God.

The Israelites were running by the light of the pillar through the sea to the other side. Once God saw that the Israelites were safe, He removed His foot from the sea. Pharaoh's army was caught in the handclap of the sea's applause to God. By the time the sea finished applauding the visit of the Creator, every Egyptian was dead and had washed ashore.

Cemetery in the Sea

At last the past was behind the Israelites. The sea that brought death to the Egyptians brought life to the Israelites. When the sea returned, it separated them from Egypt. The footprints of yesterday could never be seen again. Not only did the army of Pharaoh die there, but slavery to Egypt died there as well. God always has the last word.

Getting Out of the Past

Personal Evaluation

Read each of the following statements and answer **True** or **False**.

1. There are things in my past that hinder my personal growth. _____

2. Satan uses my past to haunt and accuse me. _____

3. I believe God can use the negative circumstances of my past as stepping-stones to promote me in my present and future. _____

4. I have total peace concerning my past. _____

5. My past has made me skeptical of people. _____

6. My past has made me fearful. _____

7. I realize I need the help of a counselor to overcome certain circumstances of my past. _____

Meditate on the following questions and answer honestly.

1. Have I truly put the past behind me?

2. What part of my past, if any, am I having trouble conquering?

3. Are there any stories I tell over and over about a certain incident that happened to me in my childhood, hoping some listening ear will unlock the door of that mental prison for me?

4. Have I turned my past over to God yet?

Group Discussion

1. Discuss what the author means by living life in the rearview mirror.

2. Could the journey through the Red Sea be considered a type of New Testament baptism? Explain.

3. Have one or two members of the group share their personal testimonies of how they overcame their past.

4. Discuss God's advice to Moses in Exodus 14:13, 14, when He told the Isrealites to stand still, see God, and hold their peace. How does this relate to our situations today?

5. Discuss the poem titled "The Cost of Character" in this chapter.

Exercise

This exercise should be done at a pond, lake, river, stream, or other large body of water. You may wish to incorporate it into a group picnic or outing.

Have the individuals in the group write on small sheets of paper the name of an individual in their past whom they have had a difficult time forgiving. They may even wish to write about a particular incident. After this is finished (privately and confidentially), give each participant a small stone or rock about the size of a softball. Now have everyone tape the paper to the rock. At this point read the story of Israel's journey through the Red Sea. At the end of the story, read Philippians 3:12-14. Now have each member of the group step forward, one at a time, and cast his stone into the deepest part of the water. As soon as this is done, have the group celebrate this victory with applause to God.

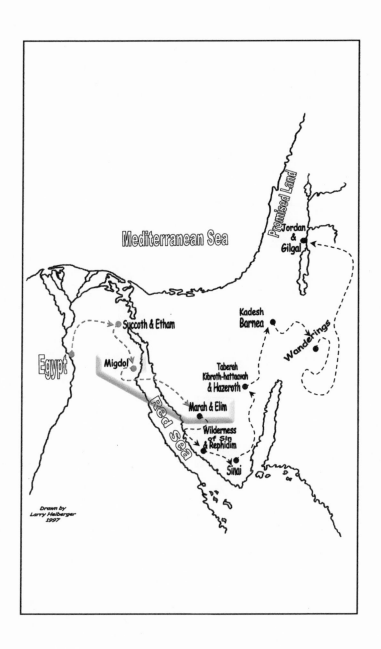

Mediterranean Sea

Promised Land

Jordan
&
Gilgal

Kadesh
Barnea

Wanderings

Succoth & Etham

Egypt

Migdol

Taberah
Kibroth-hattaavah
& Hazeroth

Red Sea

Marah & Elim

Wilderness
of Sin
& Rephidim

Sinai

Drawn by
Larry Helberger
1997

5

GETTING RID OF BITTERNESS

Camping at Marah and Elim

> *And when they came to Marah, they could not drink of the waters of Marah, for they were bitter: therefore the name of it was called Marah. And the people murmured against Moses, saying, What shall we drink? And he cried unto the Lord; and the Lord shewed him a tree, which when he had cast into the waters, the waters were made sweet: there he made for them a statute and an ordinance, and there he proved them* (Exodus 15:23-25).

Thirsty at the Brook of Bitterness

Three days without water. Anger, murmur, and frustration—these were the responses of the Israelites to their experiences during their first week in the wilderness. Little did they know that God would have them confront one of the enemies of their souls at the camp of Marah. Their parched tongues revealed an even greater fire within . . . a fire that burned deep in the reservoir of their souls.

Even though the enemy was dead, the bitter memories of Egyptian slavery were kept alive in the active files of their minds. God had removed them from their enemies, but now He must remove the disease of their souls inflicted upon them during slavery.

At last they found a brook. The sound of tumbling waters invited them. Just as they cupped their hands to drink, someone cried, "Bitter water!" Poisonous, deadly water! Enraged with fear, the people became desperate. The diseased water could not compare to the bitterness of the Israelites.

When the Better Half Becomes the Bitter Half

Bitterness! Nothing dries the taste buds like the sour taste of bitterness. Many times we react in the same way to an attitude gone bitter.

Mary Ruth and Claude (not their real names) were a typical couple who sat together on Sundays, ate at the dinner table with their four children, and played in the yard with the family dog. Their life appeared to be ideal. For the most part it was, with the exception of Claude's stressful job and Mary Ruth's obsession with worry and fear. These two problems culminated with others in a very tense marital relationship. After 15 years of marriage, eight of which were tough, Claude and Mary Ruth began to grow apart. It wasn't long before Claude began talking to a lady on his job about her troubles. Her problems made him feel useful, and his concern made her feel cared for. What began in innocence gradually turned into affection. Neither of them planned it, or even really wanted it, but it happened.

It wasn't long before Mary Ruth knew something was troubling Claude. In a matter of weeks, it all came to a head. The next few days were filled with distrustful statements, coupled with more fear. Mary Ruth and Claude eventually went to a family counselor to reconcile their relationship. Everything seemed to go well for a while, with the exceptions of Mary Ruth's suspicions and occasional accusations. The suspicions grew worse. Soon the stockpile of pain came crashing in like an avalanche. Her fears and worry escalated until she found herself in a deep emotional pit, out of control. When she finally filed for divorce, Claude begged her to reconsider. He genuinely apologized and fought desperately to save their marriage.

After the divorce, Claude moved out, and after a few years, he remarried. His leaving, however, did not seem to help Mary Ruth's behavior. She became suspicious of other people and eventually isolated herself from society. Her fears and distrust continued. Claude and their children were healed of this tragedy through prayer and counseling. Time has virtually removed all scars from their lives. Mary

Ruth, however, still lives with bitterness and distrust of everyone she meets.

How Does Bitterness Get In?

Hebrews 12:15 says: "Looking diligently lest any man fail of the grace of God; lest any root of bitterness springing up trouble you, and thereby many be defiled."

Bitterness is the cancer of the soul. It eats away your spiritual life until your once vibrant testimony is in shambles. It spreads faster than the common cold and threatens the survival of ministries, churches, families, and individuals. This scripture in Hebrews tells us that we must search our lives to see if any bitterness resides within. Note what it says—first it will trouble *you*, and then *many* will be defiled.

Bitterness usually enters through a hurt. It makes no difference if the hurt was intentional or unintentional. Bitterness is born in the womb of an unresolved offense. It may be disguised as embarrassment, disappointment, malice, or even ignorance.

The root of bitterness is detected in our emotions. Like a stamp under an infrared light, our bitterness is revealed. The hidden statements of the heart disclose the root of an embittered attitude. Bitterness justifies its residency by reasoning that the perpetrator hasn't paid for the wrong deed.

If only the victim could realize that bitterness wounds him far deeper than the person who did him wrong. It stifles self-esteem and hinders our walk with God. In Ephesians 4:31 we read, "Let all bitterness, and wrath, and anger, and clamour, and evil speaking, be put away from you, with all malice."

This passage of Scripture explains how the *seed of bitterness* grows into sin. It all begins with a hurt. That hurt turns to *wrath,* which is a seething or inner feeling of anger. Then it turns to *anger,* which occurs when the inner emotion is evident externally. Anger then graduates to *clamor,* which is foolish talking that comes from an angry soul. Clamor then turns to *evil speaking.* This is when we willfully say things designed to injure and hurt someone. The last stage is *malice,* the intent to act to harm another person.

The Bitter Truth

People who become embittered put themselves at great risk for heart disease and strokes.

Their blood pressure becomes abnormal, their respiratory system is arrested, their heart palpitations escalate, and they fall into the high-risk factor for stress-related physical ailments. In addition to the physical side effects, there are equally as many sociological side effects. Bitter people encounter a great loss of social skills that can be traced to their highly suspicious natures. They greet the world in a defensive mode, thus spoiling relationships before they have a chance to flourish. Many bitter people find it difficult to make new friends, keep old friends, and ever have a close or best friend. The tendency is to live a life of alienation.

There are also many spiritual side effects for bitter individuals. Prayer becomes difficult and is hindered because their thoughts are so embedded with doubt. Worship becomes mundane and routine because of the fear of openness and responsiveness. Faith becomes weak—almost impossible.

The psychological fallout is even worse. Bitter people see themselves as victims. Defensive and suspicious behavior often results in personality disorders. The risk of harboring bitterness is too great. It must be sought out and removed at the root.

How to Uproot Bitterness

The name *Marah* means "bitter." It wasn't mere chance that God led Israel to murky and poisoned waters. The people weren't there to find the water—they were there to find the tree. In Exodus 15:25 we read: "And he cried unto the Lord; and the Lord shewed him a tree, which when he had cast into the waters, the waters were made sweet." As the bitter waters were made sweet through the observance of this unusual and unlikely process, "there he [God] made for them a statute and an ordinance, and there he proved them." Why a tree?

The tree was a foreshadowing of the tree on which the Savior would hang thousands of years later.

God offered His name Jehovah-Rophe as a guarantee that He would heal the bitterness in the people and would serve justice on the circumstances: "If thou wilt diligently hearken to the voice of the Lord thy God, and wilt do that which is right in his sight, and wilt give ear to his commandments, and keep all his statutes, I will put none of these diseases upon thee, which I have brought upon the Egyptians: for I am the Lord that healeth thee" (Exodus 15:26). The Cross is a symbol of forgiveness; the only cure for bitterness is forgiveness.

Can I Forgive?

Getting out of the past involves the process of forgiveness. Forgiveness does not mean, "I set you free from the pain you caused me." It does not mean, "I will forget it and work to never let it happen again." Neither does it mean that the innocent absorb guilt, shame, and anger, while the guilty are let off the hook. It does not mean that you decide to excuse the wrong that was done. Forgiveness simply means this: I am relinquishing myself from the responsibility of bringing revenge on the person who did wrong. It also means that I am turning this case over to a higher court—God's court—because His Word says, "Vengeance is mine; I will repay, saith the Lord" (Romans 12:19).

The process of forgiveness is twofold:

1. Decide never to bring the offense up *against* that person again. It may be brought up as a reference, but never as an accusation.

2. Believe that God will bring justice in due season.

In chapter 4, I related the story of Jackie. She continued her therapy for several months, always coming to a point of confrontation with her past. In this case it was the perpetrator. As I led her closer to the moment of confrontation, she would say to me, "I can't forgive him for what he did."

The day finally came when I asked her to write out her contract of forgiveness and give it to me. By this time she understood that she was not justifying the individuals who did her wrong, but she was releasing herself from the responsibility of bringing judgment against them. Her contract read something like this:

Dear_____,

After a long talk with God and my counselor, I have decided to forgive you.

I know what you did to me was wrong, and I do not feel you have been repaid for it; however, I am leaving justice in the hands of God. As of this day, [_____], I will no longer be responsible for bringing judgment against you.

I forgive you and pray that you will find God in your life.

Jackie

A few weeks after this session, she wrote me a lengthy letter telling me how the power of forgiveness had totally changed her life. She even felt free to share her testimony with others a few months later, which prompted healing in the lives of others who had been abused.

Sometimes victims feel they have no future. Their hopelessness chains them to yesterday. This brings us to Ephesians 4:32: "And be ye kind one to another, tenderhearted, *forgiving one another*, even as God for Christ's sake hath forgiven you."

The Better Truth

"And they came to Elim, where were twelve wells of water, and threescore and ten palm trees: and they encamped there by the waters" (Exodus 15:27). After staying (and murmuring) at Marah three days, they traveled six miles to Elim, which means "resting place." Elim represents peace, the obvious place to overcome bitterness. The better truth is, you don't have to stay at the camp of bitterness.

One Sunday morning I spoke on the subject of bitterness. I had two of our elders bring a large 7-foot rugged cross down the aisle and place it in front of the altars. I gave the other elders a hammer and a handful of nails. That morning each person received a blank piece of paper. They were instructed to write the name of the person who had hurt them and to come and nail it on the cross. I have never seen a more powerful deliverance in an altar response. The people lined up to the back of the building and stood in line to get rid of bitterness. They found that peace was just a nail away, as illustrated in the chorus of one of my favorite songs:

Leave it there, leave it there,
Take your burden to the Lord and leave it there;
If you trust and never doubt, He will surely bring you out;
Take your burden to the Lord and leave it there.

—C. Albert Tindley

Getting Out of Bitterness

Personal Evaluation

Read each of the following statements and answer **True** or **False.**

1. I have dealt with all of the roots of bitterness in my life. _____

2. There is no one in my life I haven't forgiven. _____

3. I fully understand what it means to forgive someone. _____

4. I understand the physical, emotional, and spiritual dangers in harboring bitterness within. _____

5. I no longer hold myself responsible to bring justice to those who have wronged me. I realize that is God's job. _____

Meditate on the following questions and answer honestly.

1. Do I fully trust God to bring justice to those who have done me wrong?

2. Can I truly forgive inasmuch as I can decide never to bring up the offense against my perpetrator again?

3. Are there any hidden seeds of resentment or anger in my life that could eventually turn into bitterness?

4. Is there anyone I should go to and ask his or her forgiveness?

Group Discussion

1. Discuss the process of how anger and resentment can turn into bitterness.

2. Discuss Ephesians 4:31, 32.

3. Discuss the power of forgiveness in Matthew 6:12-15.

4. Ask a member of the group to share a personal experience of forgiveness and the changes that followed.

5. Discuss the author's two-point process of forgiveness:

a. Decide never to bring it up against that person again. It may be brought up as a reference, but never as an accusation.

b. Believe that God will bring justice in due season.

6. Discuss the danger of always seeing yourself as a victim and viewing the world through the eyes of fear. Discuss how much better it is to view yourself as an overcomer.

7. Discuss the significance of the camp of Elim, which followed Marah (Exodus 15:27).

Exercise

To do this exercise you will need the following supplies: a wooden cross, blank pieces of paper, a hammer, ink pens or pencils, and small nails.

Have the members of the group write down the names of individuals they need to forgive. Have them come, one at a time, and nail the paper to the cross. A brief moment of worship should follow to allow the Holy Spirit time to confirm the act of forgiveness and to bring peace.

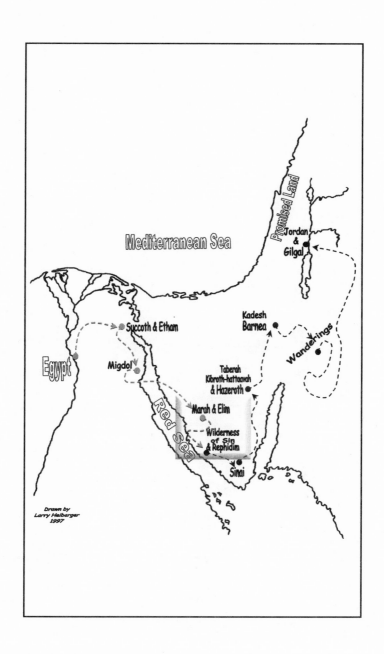

Mediterranean Sea

Promised Land

Jordan & Gilgal

Egypt

Succoth & Etham

Migdol

Kadesh Barnea

Wanderings

Red Sea

Taberah Kibroth-hattaavah & Hazeroth

Marah & Elim

Wilderness of Sin & Rephidim

Sinai

Drawn by
Larry Halberger
1997

6

GETTING RID OF MURMURING

Camping at the Wilderness of Sin and Rephidim

*Do everything without **complaining** or arguing* (Philippians 2:14, *NIV*).

*And they took their journey from Elim, and all the congregation of the children of Israel came unto the wilderness of Sin, which is between Elim and Sinai, on the fifteenth day of the second month after their departing out of the land of Egypt. And the **whole congregation of the children of Israel murmured** against Moses and Aaron in the wilderness: And the children of Israel said unto them, Would to God we had died by the hand of the Lord in the land of Egypt, when we sat by the flesh pots, and when we did eat bread to the full; for ye have brought us forth into this wilderness, to kill this whole assembly with hunger* (Exodus 16:1-3).

The Company You Keep

The trip was set. Several of us would be traveling together to a convention. We had gone out for a meal several times, but had never stayed together for any length of time. We decided to meet for breakfast to begin our day. Doug was one of the nicest guys you would ever want to meet—witty, considerate, and a good conversationalist. When we arrived for the meal, Doug and his wife, Marge (not their real names), were already there. We noticed that Marge was talking with one of the waiters about seating the group together. She seemed a little upset, but we thought she was just having a bad day. As soon as we were seated, she called for the waiter to bring a clean towel so we could reclean the table. No one really noticed the smudge, but she was greatly annoyed by it. She seemed to indicate that this was an ongoing problem for her and Doug and they had boycotted many restaurants because of it.

As the meal progressed, she refused the coffee and asked for fresh-brewed coffee. She even had one of the chairs exchanged from another table because it was dusted with a few crumbs where a child had sat earlier. Later she sent back her food to be cooked longer, and got upset with the waiter many times for his delays. By the time we left the restaurant, she was miserable and declared never to go there again. I think she is still warning people of its perils. We were in hopes that her complaints were genuine and that the rest of the trip to the convention would be less eventful.

We were not so fortunate. Each restaurant we chose had at least three or four problems, all of which were treated as major. The hotels we stayed in also had hard beds, cheap pillows, and rude service. She complained if there was a tinge of smoke, even in the hallways. We were careful not to exceed the speed limit, not to stop too frequently, not to see any sites along the way, and not to wait too late to find a good hotel in the evening. Marge didn't enjoy any of the days of travel because riding in the car made her sick. She refused to tip any of the waiters because of poor service and always filled out the complaint card at each hotel.

The rest of us tried to ignore her responses but found ourselves catering to her whims, just to keep down further complaints. Her constant complaining brought stress on the entire caravan. It goes without saying that we will not travel with her again. And you guessed it—she has complained about that too.

Marge has been complaining for years and will probably continue to do so. However, her complaining precipitated complaint among those of us who despise it. She complained about everything we did, and we all complained about her.

You become like the people who surround you. That is the power of influence. Ralph Waldo Emerson said, "You become what you think about all day." If you choose to hang out with complainers, you may eventually become one yourself.

We are not responsible for the actions of a complainer; we are only responsible for our own actions. We must decide now that associating with complainers will have negative effects. You can determine what you will be like in five years by these three things:

- The books you read
- The decisions you make
- The people with whom you associate

You cannot expect to be a positive person if all of your friends are negative. Pray this prayer with me: *Dear God, take all of the wrong people out of my life and put all the right people in.*

When you choose friends, choose them carefully. They will have either a positive or negative influence on you. It's really hard to stay encouraged when you are surrounded by discouraged people. Discouragers can change, but a person with a complaining spirit will not change until the problem is addressed through counseling or deliverance. They need to see their problem as a disease of the soul described in 2 Thessalonians 3:11, 14: "For we hear that there are some which walk among you disorderly, working not at all, but are busybodies. . . . And if any man obey not our word by this epistle, note that man, and *have no company with him*, that he may be ashamed." However, verse 15 says, "count him not as an enemy."

Bread, Birds, Brooks, and Busybodies

Can God provide a table in the wilderness? Such a limited question is inappropriate when you are talking about the Creator of the universe. The only question is, What will He provide? This story about the Wilderness of Sin and Rephidim is told quite often from the pulpit. God sends manna, quail, and water from a rock. Wow! While we are caught up in the enthusiasm of the miracle, we forget the problem the miracle alleviated.

Miracles are not for entertainment. They are not to give men a career boost. Miracles are divine interventions in life designed to "cause an effect" that will make a difference. No miracle occurs without a greater purpose. The manna, quail, and water were all miracles, but they were sent only to cure the inner cancer of complaint.

The term *wilderness of Sin* is not used in the same way the English word *sin* is used. It is simply the name of the place. It comes from the Hebrew word "*Ciyn*," which is of uncertain derivation. *Rephidim*, however, means "the bottom." God views a spirit of complaining as *reaching the bottom*. Many people have asked me, "How did I get in this shape?" How

111

does a father change from being proud of his new-born to molesting or abusing his child? How does one move from being a trusted friend to being an enemy? Going to the bottom doesn't occur in an instant. It is a downward process that starts with thinking the wrong thoughts and impulsively blurting out those thoughts. This creates a bad habit—the habit of complaining.

The Habit God Hates

Murmur comes from the Hebrew word *luwn*, which means "to stop, stay permanently, hence to be obstinate." What a fixation. Complaining will cost you progress and growth. It will stop your maturing process until you cannot relate properly to others because your paradigm of the world has become bleak and hopeless.

I am not saying that one should never complain. I am not opposed to constructive criticism. God is not angry because we have an opinion. There are times when we use the method of complaint to cor-rect wrongful circumstances. The Israelites started a downward spiral with their complaining against Moses (Exodus 16:2), which then led to complain-ing against God. The problem is not with the com-plaint; it is with the *habit of complaining*, which leads to the contamination of one's own character. The progressive steps down from a mere complaint to the habit of complaining often takes this spiritual detour, as was seen in the case of Miriam:

1. Complaining about circumstances

2. Complaining about people

3. Complaining about those with authority who are in leadership

4. Complaining against and distrusting God!

Notice what the Bible says about murmuring:

> And Moses said, This shall be, when the Lord shall give you in the evening flesh to eat, and in the morning bread to the full; for that the Lord heareth your murmurings *which ye murmur against him*: and what are we? your murmurings are not agains us, but against the Lord (Exodus 16:8). Wherefore the people did chide with Moses, and said, Give us water that we may drink. And Moses said unto them, *Why chide ye with me? wherefore do ye tempt the Lord?* (17:2).

A Rock, a River, and a Riot

The story continues. The complaining had now spread in epidemic proportions throughout the camp of the Israelites.

> And the Lord said unto Moses, Go on before the people, and take with thee of the elders of Israel; and thy rod, wherewith thou smotest the river, take in thine hand, and go.

> Behold, I will stand before thee there upon the rock in Horeb; and thou shalt smite the rock, and there shall come water out of it, that the people may drink. And Moses did so in the sight of the elders of Israel (Exodus 17:5, 6).

God was showing them the cure for complaining, but they hadn't seen it yet. Look what happened among the people while God tried to open the healing stream from the rock: "And he called the name of the place Massah, and Meribah, because of the chiding of the children of Israel, and because they tempted the Lord, saying, Is the Lord among us, or not?" (v. 7).

When God Gets Your Attention

The rock gave them water, but the miracle had no influence on their attitude. God wanted to give them the opportunity for change. John Maxwell, in his book *The Winning Attitude*, writes: "Change comes one of three ways: (1) You will change when you hurt enough that you have to change. (2) You will change when you learn enough that you want to change. (3) You will change when you receive enough that you are able to change."

So it was that God had to become the schoolmaster and Israel the pupil sent to sit in the dunce's corner. The scripture abruptly changes and these

114

terrifying words come crashing through the pages of Israel's history: "Then came Amalek *and fought with Israel in Rephidim"* (Exodus 17:8).

Out of nowhere came a battle. A people who couldn't even follow the simple directions of their leader had lost faith in their God. They became as disorganized as a newly disturbed anthill. And now a battle.

The Amalekites were descendants of Esau, and, of course, were ultimately from the seed of Abraham. It wasn't a national crisis; it was a family crisis. Look how they responded to it. Suddenly this divided band of vagrants pulled together to face the crisis. Joshua sought cooperation from every tribe (see vv. 9, 10). The things they were complaining about suddenly became insignificant.

Diagnosis of a Complainer

A great therapy for complainers is for them to ask someone who loves them to secretly write down every time they complain, to log the complaints. Then at the end of the week, sit down and review the list. The discovery is amazing. They find that most of the time they do not have strong feelings about the complaints; it is an automatic reaction to a habitual negative thought process. If you were to put a complaint under a microscope, you would most likely see the following formula:

Inconvenience + impulsive speaking + negative thinking = complaining

115

Complaining often ceases in a crisis because the individual becomes more focused on what is urgent. Not only is the inconvenience accepted, but consideration of others and their feelings takes precedence. Also, the focus changes to seeking a remedy from a negative situation to a positive one. Arguments cease when a child is hurt or someone's life is in danger. Insignificant things fade into the background, and the significant surfaces. Most habitual complaining *is* trivial and meaningless. It only detracts our focus from the important things in life.

My daughter Brittany was in an accident in 1993. I was away on a hunting trip when a farmer nearby brought me the news. That two-hour drive to the emergency room seemed like an eternity. God had my attention. I was focused on all the right things — her safety, as well as my love for her, my wife (who was there without me), and my other daughter, Lindsay. All of these were the things that I should have been focused on each day. My only response was, *Lord, I'm depending on You.*

Rephidim was stained with blood. God forgives, but many times we have to contend with the consequences of our actions. It doesn't mean we aren't forgiven; it does mean that every decision has a consequence. Choose carefully.

The Habit God Heals

Since much of the harm in a complaining spirit

116

comes from the words we say, this is where the healing must begin. It is not good enough to simply
quit saying the *wrong things*. We must start saying
the *right things*. The tool that was used as a weapon
to tear down was originally created for praise and
building up others. If you take off only the old man
without putting on the new man, you are leaving
the door open for the old man to reenter. You must
close the door to the attitude of complaint by con-
forming to your original design — praise and encouragement. Learn to say the right things. Practice saying the right things. Develop a winning vocabulary,
and ask God to help you to become an encourager.
Here are some positive and winning phrases you
can use as you develop your winning vocabulary:

- Have a great day.
- I love you.
- You are doing a good job.
- You have such a good attitude.
- You are so considerate.
- Can I do anything to help you?
- I need you.
- You are so talented.
- This is going to be a great day.
- Nothing is going to happen today that God
  and I can't handle.

A couple of years ago I was introduced to a simple little tool called "I like you because . . ." notes. Since then I have used them religiously with my staff, friends, family, and public servants. The process is simple. Create a generic card that says, "I like [person's name] because [write compliment]." Then sign your name. Here is an example:

```
I like          John
                _____

because  He is a good waiter and

smiles  all the time.  He is very

considerate to his customers.


Signed  Bryan Cutshall
```

The positive effects of this simple tool are incredible. They not only make you feel better about yourself, but they have such positive effects on the recipients. Service gets better, friendships blossom, respect level rises, and, best of all, it's a great way to let your light shine.

Practice Encouragement

Encouragement is exemplified in this story found

in Exodus 17:8-16. Moses lifted his rod and Israel prevailed against Amalek. When this 80-year-old's arms got tired and dropped to his side, Amalek prevailed. Here is where we really see the healing of the complaining spirit. Nothing conquers an ill feeling like the power of love. Moses stood summoning the angels of heaven to fight with Israel, but his worn stature was failing. He leaned upon a rock, another symbol of Christ. Suddenly, as if the master swept his brush across a canvas to bridge the portrait, it all came together. Aaron (the priest) and Hur (the Levite) ran to the top of the hill. Israel was losing. Moses was collapsing. Rephidim's valley was reeking with blood and the cries of war. The cattle were scattering. Chariots were overturning. Simultaneously, the priest grabbed one hand, the Levite the other. There was unity and victory. Amalek fled in defeat.

Disharmony turns to unity when we focus on Christ and others. The ministry of encouragement is birthed. "And Joshua discomfited Amalek and his people with the edge of the sword. . . . And Moses built an altar, and called the name of it Jehovah-nissi" (vv. 13, 15).

Jehovah-Nissi means "The Lord is my banner (flag)." You can talk about anyone you want, as long as the person you are talking to is God. Whose flag are you flying?

Getting Out of the Habit of Complaining

Personal Evaluation

Read each of the following statements and answer **True** or **False**.

1. I do not have any friends who have the habit of complaining. _____   .

2. I am in the habit of complaining. _____

3. I believe that the habit of complaining is a sin. _____

4. I believe that complaining will hinder my spiritual journey. _____

5. I have a winning vocabulary. _____

6. I am a positive thinker. _____

7. I speak more compliments than I do complaints. _____

8. I am a very complimentary individual. _____

9. I surround myself with positive, well-balanced people. _____

10. I never complain about God and the way He operates. _____

Meditate on the following questions and answer honestly.

1. Do I have a close friend who will tell me if I complain too much?

2. If I were not who I am, would I choose me to be one of my closest friends?

3. Am I in the habit of complimenting and looking for the good in people and in things?

4. Can God speak to me easily, or does He have to *get my attention*?

5. Have I chosen positive mentors to help guide me through life?

Group Discussion

1. Discuss the importance of choosing friends who are not complainers.

2. Discuss how a complaining spirit can spread like a disease among a group.

3. Discuss the kind of testimony a chronic complainer has to unbelievers.

4. Discuss how a habit of complaining will hinder your Christian growth process.

5. Discuss what it means to have a winning vocabulary.

6. Discuss John Maxwell's three statements on change:

   a. You will change when you hurt enough that you have to change.

   b. You will change when you learn enough that you want to change.

   c. You will change when you receive enough that you are able to change.

7. Ask each person to describe how he or she feels after leaving the presence of a chronic complainer.

8. Discuss what kind of message a complaining spirit is sending to God.

Exercise

Before the class begins, make up several "I like you because . . ." cards.

Give the members of the group several "I like you because . . ." cards and ask them to use them all before the next class time. Begin the next class by giving testimonies of the impact this positive gesture had on the recipients.

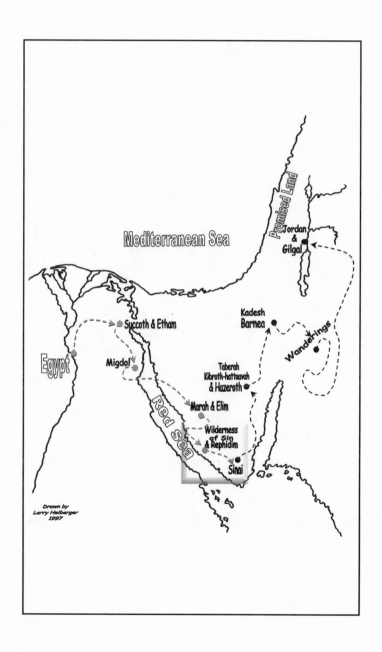

Mediterranean Sea

Promised Land

Jordan & Gilgal

Kadesh Barnea

Wanderings

Egypt

Succoth & Etham

Migdol

Red Sea

Taberah
Kibroth-hattaavah
& Hazeroth

Marah & Elim

Wilderness
of Sin
& Rephidim

Sinai

Drawn by
Larry Helberger
1997

7

GETTING RID OF DOUBT

Camping at Mount Sinai

In the third month, when the children of Israel were gone forth out of the land of Egypt, the same day came they into the wilderness of Sinai (Exodus 19:1).

Is He Really There or Not?

Barbara (not her real name) was raised in church. As a little girl she went to Sunday school and Vacation Bible School in her small independent church. Her church attendance was somewhat regular considering her family's instability. When things would go wrong, her family would just move on. Because of this, her father became more of a pastor to her than anyone else. Years passed and Barbara eventually married. She and her husband raised a beautiful family and attended church once or twice a month.

One morning about 6:00 my phone rang. On the

125

other end, Barbara was sobbing as though her world had come to an end. Through her tears she asked, "How could God let these things keep happening to me?" I prayed with her and asked her to meet me at my office later that day. As I began to probe into her knowledge of God, I found a lady who had an extremely distorted view of God. Her relationship with God was built on fear rather than love. Her view of God was more that of a dictatorial landlord. In the hour when she really needed Him, she doubted His love, His care for her, and even His existence.

Barbara is typical of many who go to church but never truly go to God. They sing His songs but do not understand what they are singing. They are very religious, but not very spiritual. They have a moderate level of commitment to the church, but they do not have a personal relationship with God. The creature and the Creator have never really communed. Worship, therefore, was inconsequential and sermons had little impact.

Barbara's problem was doubt. The opposite of doubt is trust. You can trust only when you truly know an individual. An antonym for *doubt* is *faith*. When we have faith, we do not doubt. The Bible says, "Without faith it is impossible to please God; for when we come to God, we must believe that He exists and that He wants to reward those who seek Him with all their heart" (Hebrews 11:6, paraphrased).

A Visit From God

Three months had passed since the Israelites left Egypt. At Mount Sinai they set up camp for the next 11 months and five days. This was the place where Moses was visited by God in the burning bush months earlier (Exodus 3). Sinai was the mountainous region, and Horeb was the name of one particular mountain in that region.

The story opens with Moses drawing a boundary line around the mountain base (19:12). Any person or animal trespassing the line would die. The people were instructed to wash themselves on the third day in order to "be ready" for a visit from God (v. 11). The anticipated third day came with a display that would make our most ornate fireworks look like a backyard Fourth of July celebration. A thick cloud rested on the mountain. From the cloud came a pompous fanfare of thundering, accompanied by heaven's own laser show of lightning bolts and enchanting light explosions. All of this seemed to be conducted by an overture of trumpet blasts. Smoke billowed skyward and the mountain shook profusely as God began to speak audibly to the company of Israelites. The people listened fearfully to the hallowed oration. Afterward, they pleaded with Moses to speak for them because the scene was too frightening (20:19). Moses then agreed to approach the cloud alone.

Moses remained on the mountain for 40 days

(24:18). At some time during this period, God inscribed the Ten Commandments on two tablets of stone. On the 40th day, God told Moses that the people had sinned by making a golden calf (ch. 32). This was done because the people couldn't see Moses and presumed he was dead. They *could "see" God* on the mountain, but they *couldn't see Moses.* The display of God's presence was still there. The truth is they looked to Moses as their leader rather than to God. In reality, Moses had become their God. Their inability to see Moses prompted them to create another god to worship.

How Does Doubt Get Into Our Spirit?

1. *We get our eyes off God and get them on man* (see Exodus 32:1). Man is certainly the representative of God, but he is never a substitute for God.

A few years ago a lady came to my office declaring that she was leaving the church and Christianity. She was convinced that all Christians were hypocrites and all ministers were liars. She continued to fume about churches becoming more concerned about money than they were about souls.

After she vented her anger, she began to cry. Her real problem was that her favorite evangelist had been exposed as a moral failure. His crisis had capsized her faith. She eventually realized that he too was a man. She concluded that she held him so high on a pedestal that she never prayed for him. She

128

took so much from his ministry and never stopped to think what he needed from his followers to maintain his own level of faith. The tug of the crowd finally became too hard for him. She had to realize that her faith was in God, not in a man. God had not failed.

2. *We get our eyes on circumstances instead of on God.* All that the Israelites could see was the present. God had them there for a purpose. He never intended for them to remain there, but they got their eyes off the goal — Canaan. When you get your eyes off the destination, all you can see are your present surroundings.

We all have bad days, but that doesn't mean we have to concede to having a bad life. I have a saying that I use around the office when things aren't going well: "It's only a day, it's not a life." We must become removed from the circumstances and our emotions to accurately assess the situation.

3. *We get self-centered instead of God-centered.* Life just doesn't seem to move fast enough for most of us. It is easy to get so locked-in to our own philosophy and goals that we forget God's agenda.

We have always been torn between the will of God and our own will. We need to find the place where our will and God's will become one. God has given man free will to choose the routes of life. Many mistakenly believe God's will is a type of albatross or burden.

The key to God's will is found in the talents and interests He places within us. His will is not a magnetic force vying for our time and energies. The struggle of man was never intended to be with the will of God but rather with the desires of the flesh. Finding God's will thrusts us toward life's fullest capabilities and potentials.

4. *We surround ourselves with doubters.* Aaron and the elders had been on the mountain with God. It was easy to have faith while being surrounded by the "saints" who were having visions. But now Aaron had become influenced by the doubters. His faith was replaced by discouragement when he left the mountain. Today we can't always live on the mountain. It is our responsibility to remember in the dark what God told us in the light.

Doubters are threatened by anyone who has vision and faith. Doubt steals our dreams, faith, and vision. Every group has one or more doubters. Doubters come in all sizes and ages, but their mission is the same — to convince you of 90 reasons why it can't be done. They seem to have detectors for all the things that *might* go wrong. They call themselves realists or conservatives, but the truth is, "The just shall live by faith" (Romans 1:17), and that is a foreign concept to them. They seem to know all the people who have tried and failed. They are prophets of doom. Their focus is singular, their risks are few, their fate is inevitable, their dreams are limited, and their faith is futile. These are the doubters.

FAITH VS. DOUBT

Faith is always part of the answer;
Doubt is always part of the problem.

Faith always has a program;
Doubt always has an excuse.

Faith always says, "Let me do it for you";
Doubt says, "You're doing it wrong."

Faith sees an answer for every problem;
Doubt sees a problem for every answer.

Faith sees a green near every sand trap;
Doubt sees two or three sand traps near every
green.

Faith says, "It may be difficult, but it's possible";
Doubt says, "It may be possible, but it's too difficult."

Walk by faith!

— *Author unknown*

The Quest to See God!

The pessimistic and immature statement "When I see it, I'll believe it" is made too often. These people are saying to God, "Show it to me and I'll believe." However, God says, "Believe and I'll show

131

it to you." The disease of doubt can only be cured by a dose of *trust* and *faith*. Before trust is possible, a personal relationship with God must exist. Faith is a by-product of trusting God. We must see God for ourselves in order to trust and believe Him. The following three steps will help us to begin our own personal journey with God.

1. *We need to understand how God thinks.* God's thoughts are written in His Word. It is extremely important for us to own a version of the Bible that we can understand. God cannot speak to us if we don't understand what He is saying. God's Word must be relevant.

2. *We need to communicate with God.* This is done through prayer and meditation. Prayer should be comfortable and consistent. I suggest you block out time each morning to spend with God. Having praise choruses or slow, sacred music in the background creates an atmosphere for prayer. Begin by thanking Him for all His blessings in your life. You will be surprised how it will bring you into a positive frame of mind before you start the day. I suggest you write down your prayer requests and either read the list or remind yourself that God knows your needs before you ask Him. Spend most of your time in prayer getting to know God. After a time of thanking Him, you may wish to worship. Many people do not understand the difference between *praise* and *worship*. The terms are not synonymous. *Praise* is thanking God for

132

what He has done. Worship is placing value on God for *who He is.*

Ecclesiastes 5:1, 2 tells us to listen to Him rather than to speak. Solomon writes that we should just stand in awe of God and not be hasty with our words. When we spend time with God, our minds have a tendency to wander, organizing the activities of our day. Having a pen and pad nearby will usually remedy this hindrance. When a thought comes to you, write it down and return to your mode of worship.

3. *We need to serve God.* "They that wait upon the Lord shall renew their strength" (Isaiah 40:31). The word *wait* in this passage has the connotation of a *waiter* or *waitress.* It implies that we serve while waiting on God. This is accomplished by doing things for others in the name of God. When we do things for the underprivileged, we are doing things for the Lord (Matthew 25:40).

The Touch of His Hand—All Doubt Is Gone!

The disobedience of the Israelites brought discouragement to Moses. In a tent, outside the Hebrew camp, Moses privately communed with God. Then God led Him to a rock and told him to stand upon that rock. "I will place my hand over you," God said (see Exodus 33:21, 22). What a safe place to be . . . under God's hand. His touch removes our

133

doubts. Counseling is a wonderful tool, but it is limited without the touch of God. Preaching can be stimulating, but preaching alone cannot change a life without the touch of God. A song is not a psalm unless the touch of God is on it. A lesson is not a teaching unless it has the touch of God. A sermon is not a message without the touch of God.

This is not a carnal journey, but a spiritual one. Our spirit is reaching for the source from which it came. It is not a question of God's passing by. Rather, it is a question of our reaching out to touch Him. His presence fills the universe. One touch and doubt will dissipate. But be prepared—your spirit will long to touch Him time and time again. You will long to get away and sit in the cleft of the rock, to see Him with your spiritual eyes and feel Him brush by you in all of His glory. If doubt returns, go back to the rock and touch Him again. He'll be waiting.

Getting Out of Doubt

Personal Evaluation

Read each of the following statements and asnwer **True** or **False.**

1. I sometimes doubt the existence of God. _____

2. I have a *personal* relationship with God. _____

3. I do not hold God responsible for men's failures and mistakes. _____

4. I have not surrounded myself with doubters. _____

5. I have regular and meaningful communication with God. _____

6. I am a faithful worker in the kingdom of God. _____

7. I live by faith. _____

Meditate on the following questions and answer honestly.

1. Am I more convinced of the existence of Satan than I am of the existence of God?

2. Do I see God properly?

3. Have I allowed myself to become discouraged by the failures and mistakes of men and women who represent God?

4. Do I consider myself to be a good example of a Christlike person?

5. Am I out of focus in any area of my Christian walk?

Group Discussion

1. Discuss the case study of Barbara at the beginning of chapter 7. Ask the group to analyze how Barbara could stay in church for so many years and know so little about the Bible and God.

2. Discuss Hebrews 11:6 as it relates to believing in the existence of God.

3. Discuss the setting of Mount Sinai in Exodus 19 and try to determine why the people made the golden calf after witnessing such an awesome sight.

4. Discuss the four statements relating to how doubt gets into our spirit:

    a. We get our eyes off God and get them on a man.

    b. We get our eyes on circumstances instead of on God.

    c. We get self-centered instead of God-centered.

    d. We surround ourselves with doubters.

5. Discuss the poem "Faith vs. Doubt."

6. Discuss the maxim that says, "Give God what's in your hand and He will give you what's in His."

7. Have a member of the group relate a personal experience about doubt and tell how he/she overcame it.

8. Read the image God paints of Himself in Job 38–41 and discuss it.

Exercise

Have the members of the group describe how they see God. This will be a powerful faith-building exercise which will stimulate the mind and spirit of those who participate. During each person's description, ask the other members of the group to close their eyes so they may fully concentrate and get the impact of the exercise.

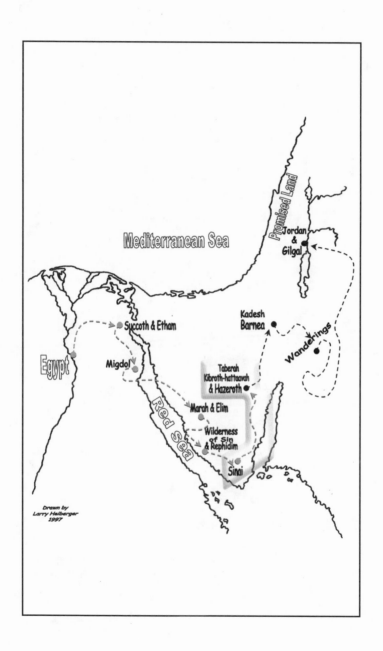

Mediterranean Sea

Promised Land

Jordan & Gilgal

Kadesh Barnea

Wanderings

Succoth & Etham

Egypt

Migdol

Taberah
Kibroth-hattaavah
& Hazeroth

Red Sea

Marah & Elim

Wilderness of Sin & Rephidim

Sinai

Drawn by
Larry Halberger
1997

8

GETTING RID OF STRESS

Camping at Taberah, Kibroth-hattaavah, and Hazeroth

And when the people complained, it displeased the Lord: and the Lord heard it; and his anger was kindled; and the fire of the Lord burnt among them, and consumed them that were in the uttermost parts of the camp. And the people cried unto Moses; and when Moses prayed unto the Lord, the fire was quenched. And he called the name of the place Taberah: because the fire of the Lord burnt among them (Numbers 11:1-3).

Sizzling Saints in a Pressure Cooker World

As a young boy I remember coming into the house and hearing the sound of the old pressure cooker. It was a large pot with a tightly fitted lid. When the pot heated up, the pressure was trapped inside, thus pressuring the food. On top was an apparatus we called the "sizzler." The job of the sizzler was to keep the pressure from building up too high, causing the pot to explode.

Stress builds up in our lives in the very same way the pressure builds in the pot. If the sizzler ever failed, the pot would explode. If we don't cope with stress, the same thing can happen to us. An overload of stress also leads to burnout. The following are symptoms of stress as well as some of the early stages of burnout:

- Constant dissatisfaction
- Restlessness
- Persistent fatigue
- Irritability (short fuse)
- Memory lapse
- Frustration with the progress of life

The phrase *stressed out* may be described like this: "The emotional well has run dry, the physical motor is out of oil, and spiritual strength is depleted." Emotional downers create a syndrome of self-criticism, self-doubt, and self-pity. Spiritually, we are prone to question God, discount His will, reject His Word, and refuse to utilize His resources.

Stress overload keeps us from focusing properly on life and on God. It robs us of our benevolent nature and replaces it with self-centeredness. With the focus on self, we become easily offended and have a tendency to read the wrong message into circumstances.

Stress can cause you to walk through life with blinders on. Recently I read that horses have the largest eyes of any animal except the ostrich. Their eyes are located on the sides of their heads, permitting them to see two different directions at once. However, they do have a hard time seeing in front of their body. This is their blind spot. So it is with the stressed-out individual who is focused on the side issues but is blinded to the things right in front.

My friend Jerry O'Bryan was diagnosed several years ago with Crohn's disease. This incurable disease caused attachments to form inside his body like a spider's web between the internal organs. Once attached, the strawlike channels allow secretions to escape from one vital organ and flow into another. Treatment for this disease is complicated because it is not localized.

Stress moves through the spirit of man in the same way that Crohn's disease moves through the body—entangling itself with our faith and other spiritual faculties. Because of too much stress, our spiritual vision may become distorted and our sensitivity to the leading of God calloused.

Burned Out but Still Born Again

The stress of life takes the sizzle out of many great leaders whose days are filled with long hours of ministry. But thank God, we can be burned out and

143

still be born again. Because of the busy schedule, the many complaints, and the heavy problems ministers encounter, burnout accelerates. It is easy to forget who the real audience is. The audience is not the people; the audience is God. And we are not the star; Jesus is the star. All we do is run the spotlight.

Moses learned that leadership without delegation produced bottlenecks. He was feeling the effects of burnout when God told him to choose 70 elders to oversee the people. God told Moses that He would come down in a cloud and "take of" the Spirit that was on Moses and put on each of the elders. When this happened, they went throughout the camp prophesying (see Numbers 11:16-25).

Stress in Leadership

Leadership is a breeding ground for jealousy and competition unless you are promoted through the ranks of "followship." Two men by the names of Eldad and Medad were prophesying in the camp instead of at the Tabernacle. A young man came to Moses complaining because that wasn't the way they always did it. Just as some forget the difference in organization and formalization, this young man was missing the point. He thought they were supposed to be religious. Moses said, "No, they are supposed to be spiritual." In fact, Moses said that he wished he had more like them (see vv. 26-30).

144

Being different does not mean you are wrong. Many are judged for doing things in a different fashion. God chose to use John the Baptist, a wild, unshaven hermit. He also chose a hotheaded Peter who denied Him. He chose a harlot in the city of Jericho and a disobedient prophet named Jonah to go to Nineveh. God uses the ordinary to do the extraordinary. God uses the ridiculous to perform the miraculous. The critics of leaders are found in every arena.

In addition to handling the complaints of the people, Moses also dealt with jealousy from his own brother and sister because God wasn't speaking through them to the people (see Numbers 12). Miriam and Aaron began to bicker, in a sense, over titles. They were jealous of Moses' position with God. Miriam said, "Has God chosen to only speak through you? He speaks through us too! We want to be the leaders for a while." God smote Miriam with leprosy, but Moses interceded for her. However, God caused her to be put out of the camp for seven days.

John Maxwell, in *Developing the Leader Within You*, writes: "Leadership is not a position, it is influence." Don't demand respect and followership simply because of your position. Lead by example, and let your followers come after you. Titles mean nothing if we are not doing the job.

It doesn't matter what you are called as long as

you are doing the job. Jealousy is a killer. It will rob you of friendships, influence, and your personal testimony.

Beating Burnout and Stamping Out Stress

Here is a formula for beating stress:

1. Build the body.
2. Manage the mind.
3. Stabilize the self.
4. Assess your gifts.
5. Relish your relationships.
6. Balance your behavior.

Build the body. First we must build our bodies, realizing that our bodies are the epitome of God's creation. To abuse our bodies is to discredit the creation of God. To care for and build up our bodies is to present them unto the Lord as worship. Regular exercise is a vital weapon for controlling stress. "'Breaking a sweat' on a regular basis through meaningful, and hopefully enjoyable, exercise lowers the anxiety level and clears the mind," states Dr. Paul L. Walker. Before we ask God to remove our stresses, we must realize that it is our responsibility to get our bodies in shape.

Manage the mind. Some people are stressed because they listen to the wrong people and the wrong things. About 50 percent of their stress could be alleviated by eliminating the time spent on the phone with negative people and by carefully choosing the things they read. Be selective and make sure that a proper dosage of the *right* stuff is going in every day. A good question to ask is this: What kind of positive information do you feed your mind each day, and is it enough to balance all the negative information you will hear?

Stabilize the self. One of our greatest problems with stress is that we put more pressure on ourselves than we should. We have a big "image" problem in our country, worrying about what others think and say about us. There is a fun therapy to help you discover a little more about yourself. It is a simple, old-fashioned image-association test. First, you think of a color. You must then write down three words that describe that color. Next, you write down the name of your favorite animal. Then write three words that describe that animal.

How does it work? The first set of three words describes how you truly are on the inside. The second set of three words describes how you want others to view you. We subconsciously choose colors and animals that we can relate to. There is something about those choices that reveals a part of the inward self. It is important to understand your strengths and weaknesses, as well as your temperament. Knowing these things about yourself will enable you to lead a less stressful life.

Assess your gifts. One thing the clergy has had to deal with in the last decade is the question of professionalism. We were told to break out of the country-preacher mode to become more equipped to teach, and to hone our administrative skills. Now many find themselves asking these questions: Are we counselors or preachers? Administrators or shepherds? Teachers or businessmen?

Unfortunately, the demand is to be all of the above. I attended a pastors conference last year where a layman spoke on what the laity wanted from their pastors. He listed the following things:

1. Administrator

2. Businessman

3. Marketer

4. Public relations man

5. Psychologist/counselor

6. Master of Ceremonies

7. Accountant

8. Building contractor

9. Balanced example of physical fitness

10. Family person

11. Spiritual leader

12. One who shows high accountability on all levels of job performance

13. Personal developer of all ministries

14. One who shares the responsibilities of lay-men

He continued by saying, "I expect my pastor to pray every day; be respectful, supportive, and on call when I need him. I expect him to have a vast knowledge of God's Word, to love, and to give of his time and finances." He concluded, "He must be a learner, advance to higher levels of learning, and work for reasonable pay."

I was surprised that he didn't include "More powerful than a locomotive, faster than a speeding bullet, and able to leap tall buildings at a single bound"! One of our problems with stress is that we think we have to be great at everything. My advice is to know your limitations, staff your weaknesses, and work within the parameters of your strengths. Relax.

Relish relationships. Some stress is caused by never learning the value and talents of those around you. Therefore, we try to fill a void by chasing ghosts of every whim and fancy. Learn the truly valuable things in life, and leave off some of the things that are insignificant.

- Learn the value of family — never take it for granted.

- Learn the value of marriage — never abuse it.

149

- Learn the value of God—keep Him near you always.

- Learn the value of children—take time to laugh and play with them.

- Learn the value of friends—pursue time together.

- Learn the value of purity—make it a personal goal.

- Learn the value of pleasures—they were put here for a purpose.

Stress is increased when we fail to draw strength from others. People are blessings. The truth is, no one has to like you, but the people who do like you, choose to do so of their own free will. Cherish them.

Balance your behavior. Wrong behavior causes guilt, not release! Right behavior is a choice before it is a habit. It doesn't matter who is right, it is *what is right* that counts. We must make the choice to think the right thoughts. Right thoughts produce right actions, not the other way around. A balanced behavior is one that is not overdone in any one area. It is an attitude that is flexible and surrendered to the work and person of the Holy Spirit—a behavior distinctly different from those committed to this world's system. A balanced individual exemplifies the fruit of the Spirit, denoting that God is in control. A balanced behavior begins with a choice to right behavior, right thinking, and a right relationship with God.

Getting Out of Stress

Personal Evaluation

Read each of the following statements and answer **True** or **False.**

1. I have a problem managing stress. _____

2. I take the complaints of others too personally. _____

3. I get the proper amount of exercise. _____

4. I draw strength from my relationship with my family. _____

5. My thoughts dwell more on the positive than the negative. _____

6. I like who I am and do not feel like I have an image problem. _____

7. I properly manage the things my mind feeds on. _____

8. I pray for temperance and patience. _____

9. I feel that I live my life in balance. _____

10. I have a positive friend I can call when I feel stressed out. _____

151

Meditate on the following questions and answer honestly.

1. Do I have my priorities in order concerning my relationships with family and friends?

2. Do I expect too much of myself and others?

3. Do I let little things get to me?

4. Do I take good care of my body?

5. Do I know who the audience is?

Group Discussion

1. Discuss the importance of living a balanced life.

2. Discuss the phrase "burned out but still born again." What does the author mean by this phrase?

3. Discuss creative and practical ways to do the following things:

   a. Build your body.

   b. Manage your mind.

   c. Stabilize yourself.

   d. Assess your gifts.

   e. Relish your relationships.

   f. Balance your behavior.

4. Ask a member of the group to share a personal experience of being overstressed and give a report of how he/she overcame it.

Exercise

Have the members of the group to stand and form a single line. Next have them place their hands on the shoulders of the person in front of them. Ask them to massage their neck and shoulders. Have them now to turn and face the opposite direction and do the same thing again.

This exercise will be fun as well as relaxing. You may even wish to conclude with an invigorating group walk around the block to really put into action the things you have studied.

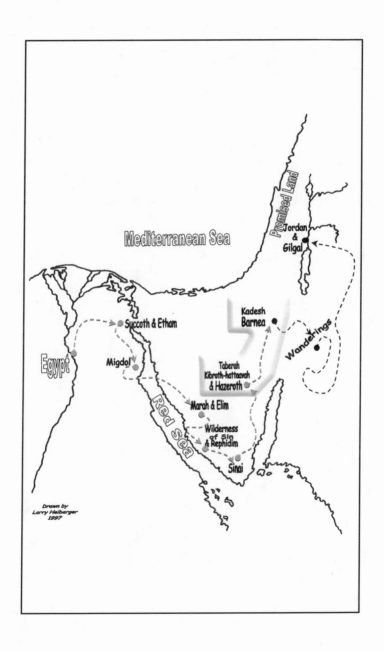

9

GETTING RID OF FEAR

Camping at Kadesh Barnea

And the Lord spake unto Moses, saying, Send thou men, that they may search the land of Canaan, which I give unto the children of Israel: of every tribe of their fathers shall ye send a man, every one a ruler among them. And Moses by the commandment of the Lord sent them from the wilderness of Paran: all those men were heads of the children of Israel. . . . And Moses sent them to spy out the land of Canaan, and said unto them, Get you up this way southward, and go up into the mountain: and see the land, what it is; and the people that dwelleth therein, whether they be strong or weak, few or many; and what the land is that they dwell in, whether it be good or bad; and what cities they be that they dwell in, whether in tents, or in strong holds; and what the land is, whether it be fat or lean, whether there be wood therein, or not. And be ye of good courage, and bring of the fruit of the land. Now the time was

*the time of the firstripe grapes. . . . And they
came unto the brook of Eshcol, and cut down from
thence a branch with one cluster of grapes, and
they bare it between two upon a staff; and they
brought of the pomegranates, and of the figs. . . .
And they returned from searching of the land after
forty days. And they went and came to Moses,
and to Aaron, and to all the congregation of the
children of Israel, unto the wilderness of Paran,
to Kadesh; and brought back word unto them,
and unto all the congregation, and shewed them
the fruit of the land* (Numbers 13:1-3, 17-26).

The Edge of Victory

Feel the wind in your face, the spring in your
heels, and the taste of triumph on your lips. This is
the feeling you get seconds before crossing the finish line. Victory sings the praises of a job well done,
a long-awaited medallion, and the thrill of the conquest. Perhaps those few seconds on the edge make
up for the years of training and scores of sacrifices
for which there are no records, only scars.

"No pain, no gain," we keep saying. So we press
on, knowing that victory is achievable. Vince
Lombardi once said, "It's not whether you get
knocked down, it's whether you get up." Success
is getting back up one more time than you get
knocked down. It's the edge of victory that keeps
us in the race when we feel like quitting.

Zadok Robinowitz says, "A man's dreams are

an index to his greatness." It is his dreams that make him feel alive. Basil S. Walsh wrote, "If you don't know where you are going, how can you expect to get there?" Many people are getting nowhere in life simply because they aren't headed any specific place.

At last the Promised Land was in sight. The mountains of Hebron and the Valley of Eshcol never looked so good. These wanderers were almost home. Their faces were dry and ruddy from the year and six months of desert living. Their mouths watered for the familiar taste of herbs, garlic, and leeks. Their menu of manna, quail, and occasional food from the land was getting old. Children dreamed of playing in the pools of Gibeon and Heshbon. The aged could finally rest by sitting in the shade of the poplars and enjoying the taste of ripe olives, figs, and fresh bread. The women visualized new grains and oils for baking. The men thought of rich land for planting and harvesting.

The nights now ended with endless chatter from children who had high hopes of a land of milk and honey. For the moment, complaining had ceased and hope filled the hearts of the eager travelers. At last the long period of testing would be over. The only thing left was to pass God's final exam.

Miracles and Faith

Many people assume that if God showed them a

miracle, it would change their lives forever. Miracles do not produce faith; faith produces miracles. The children of Israel saw the sea part, manna fall from heaven, water flow from a rock, millions of quail delivered by the wind, healing of all sorts, and clothes and shoes that never wore out. They heard God's audible voice, saw His presence each day in the pillar of cloud and fire, and saw His presence on the mountain with Moses and the 70 elders. They saw the plagues afflict Egypt, the earth swallow the complainers, and God smite the Amalekites. All of this happened in just 18 months. Surely they must have had incredible faith in the abilities and faithfulness of God. What could possibly hinder this kind of faith?

The greatest hindrance to faith is not the absence of God's power. The greatest hindrance to the Israelites' faith, and to our faith today, is a four-letter word—*fear*.

- Faith is the force that activates God's power in our lives.

- Fear is the force that activates Satan's power in our lives.

The Grasshopper Syndrome

At God's command, Moses chose a man from each of the 12 tribes to spy out the land (Numbers 13:3-15). The spies covered the territory from

160

Kadesh at the southern tip of the Desert of Zin, to Rehob at the northern tip and back (a round trip of approximately 500 miles). Anticipation was running high throughout the camp. They stood on the threshold of promise or peril. Children ran through the camp clamoring the news that the 12 were back from their mission. At the sound of the shofar, the people gathered to hear the report. You could hear a pin drop as the spies testified to the richness of the land. They even brought clusters of grapes that took two men to carry. The land was everything God promised — everything, that is, except achievable.

While on the journey they saw men of great stature. Their hearts were pricked with fear. They proclaimed, "We were like grasshoppers in their sight" (see Numbers 13:31-33). Scripture does not say that the giants called them grasshoppers. This is what they called themselves. Fear caused them to see themselves differently. Two of the spies, however, Joshua and Caleb, perceived things quite differently — they were confident and determined.

- Ten came back complaining and two came back conquering.
- Ten came back grumbling and two came back gratified.
- Ten came back chiding and two came back challenged.
- Ten came back horrified and two came back hopeful.

- Ten came back oppressed and two came back overcomers.

The Revelation of Character

The way you see yourself determines the level of fear or faith that can operate in your life. These 18 months in the desert were not to show them who God was; it was to show them who they were. God had to get them to stop thinking like slaves.

The purpose of the wilderness training camp was to reveal character. John Wooden wrote, "Be more concerned with your character than your reputation. Your character is what you really are, while your reputation is merely what others think you are." The trials of life are there to bring out our latent qualities, not to fill us with the fear of defeat. Imagine 2.5 million people eating angel-baked bread and God-delivered quail and drinking miracle water . . . still feeling like grasshoppers. Before conquering the enemy, who you think is the source of your fear, you must conquer your greatest enemy — yourself.

The Remedy for Fear Is Courage

Fear refines courage, and courage takes us across the finish line. Being afraid does not mean we are going to lose. A popular slogan on the back of sports attire says, "No Fear." To approach life without any fear is to live in denial. The goal is to approach life with the assurance that we can conquer our fears. Eddie Rickenbacker writes, "Courage is doing what you're afraid to do. There can be no courage unless you're scared."

Mark Twain said, "Courage is resistance to fear and mastery of fear—not absence of fear." Fear keeps us from even trying. Elbert Hubbard said, "The greatest mistake a man can make is to be afraid of making one."

The Battle of the Giants

Before you can understand the faith of Joshua and Caleb, you must know that they too were "giants." In a physical sense, a giant is simply a man with an oversized body. However, the body is only part of a man. The whole person consists of a body, soul, and spirit. You can be a physical giant and a spiritual dwarf. In the case of Joshua and Caleb, however, they were spiritual giants.

As each of the spies gave his report, the people began to squirm. Their faith was sinking. They could feel fear swelling. It began with a chatter. Then one negative statement bred another. Mothers clinched their children tightly each time one of the spies repeated the word *giant*. Old men dropped to the ground in despair. The commotion heightened to a roar as the negativism spread through the tribes. They whispered at first, then shouted, "What are we going to do now? We told you Moses was a

163

fraud. God is punishing us. We are going to die!" (see Numbers 14:1-3).

Joshua and Caleb spoke, but the angry crowd could not hear them. Finally, they stood before the people and ripped their clothes, screaming, "Listen, people, listen." Several minutes passed before the mob became quiet. They alluded to the cities waiting for them and that the giants would be as bread to them. They urged the people to trust God and not to fear, but their pleas went unheeded (vv. 6-9).

Your Problem Is Not Your Problem

John C. Maxwell, in his book *Be All You Can Be*, declares, "Your problem is not your problem; it's the way you handle your problem that is your problem." The problem was not the report. The problem was not the land. Everything God had promised was there. The problem was fear.

There will come a time in each of our lives when we have to walk by faith. We see the possibilities, but the problems seem *larger than we are*. Problems of this magnitude require trusting a higher power. Give them to God. There is no shame in admitting that we need God's help. He is the deliverer.

Obstacles or Opportunities

The Chinese language is composed of characters which form words. The Chinese word for *crisis* is made up of two Chinese characters: *wei*, meaning "danger" and *ji*, meaning "opportunity." Thus the Chinese view a crisis not as two separate realities but as two sides of the same reality, containing both danger and opportunity. It only becomes tragedy if we fail to see the opportunity. Consider the following Biblical examples:

- Joseph went through the dungeon to get to the king's palace.

- David went through the battlefield to get to the throne.

- Joshua went through the wilderness to get to Canaan.

Promotion often comes through problem situations. Every solution that exists comes to us because of a problem. Some Christians have the mistaken concept that Christians do not have problems. However, we have the same circumstances arise in our lives as the non-Christians. The difference is in how we handle them. If we choose to handle them the same way as the non-Christians, we get the same results. If we allow God to direct us in handling our problems, He can turn a tragedy into a triumph.

Rejecting God

The Israelites reacted in such a way that God had to step in (Numbers 14:10). Their fury rose to the point that they wanted to get rid of Moses, stone Joshua and Caleb, and go back to Egypt. As they were getting ready to collect the stones, God showed up. The Shekinah cloud came out of the Tabernacle, and God spoke to the people. The 10 spies who gave the negative report were smitten with a deadly plague (vv. 36, 37).

The people trembled as God pronounced judgment on them. In verses 29-34, He declared that they would wander one year for every day the spies searched out the land. They were gone 40 days, so a sentence of 40 years was handed down. The people left the camp of Kadesh in defeat. God declared that everyone over the age of 20 years would die in the next 40 years, with the exceptions of Joshua and Caleb.

What a tragedy! Approximately 1.2 million men and women would die during this period of time. Individual burials would have required 85 funerals daily. If there were 12 hours of daylight, they would have conducted seven funerals every hour of the day. This perhaps was the first "Trail of Tears."

A quote by Henry Ford may apply here: "Whether you think you can or think you can't— you are right."

Getting Out of Fear

Personal Evaluation

Read each of the following statements and answer **True** or **False**.

1. I sometimes feel like giving up when I'm stressed.

   _____

2. Sometimes my fear hinders my faith. _____

3. Fear has changed the way I see myself. _____

4. I am a courageous person. _____

5. Fear has robbed me of good opportunities.

   _____

6. I realize there is opportunity in every obstacle.

   _____

7. I truly believe God wants me to live in victory.

   _____

167

Meditate on the following questions and answer honestly.

1. At the level of faith on which I am operating now, which group of spies would I have most likely sided with—the 10 spies who gave the bad report or the two who gave the good report?

2. Do I overreact to situations and create problems for myself?

3. Do I see myself as a spiritual giant or a spiritual grasshopper?

4. Am I easily intimidated? (If the answer to this is yes, please read Ezekiel 2.)

Group Discussion

1. Discuss the following two statements:

    a. Faith is the force that activates God's power in our lives.

    b. Fear is the force that activates Satan's power in our lives.

2. Discuss the subject of courage, using the following statements as guidelines:

    a. Fear refines courage.

    b. Courage takes us across the finish line.

    c. Courage is doing what you're afraid to do.

There can be no courage unless you're scared.

3. Discuss the following statement on character: "Your character is what you really are, while your reputation is merely what others think you are."

4. Discuss the promise of God to give the Israelites a land flowing with milk and honey, and decide whether the group feels that God kept His part of the promise.

5. Have a member of the group share a personal experience when a crisis offered two roads — one that led to opportunity and the other that led to tragedy.

Exercise

This group project will last for one week. The project assignment is to collect "good reports" for an entire week. It will take some effort, but the results will be both positive and rewarding. Group members should simply interview people who have "good news" to share. Write out the reports or have others to write it out for them. In the next group meeting, read the good reports that have been collected. This exercise is a faith builder.

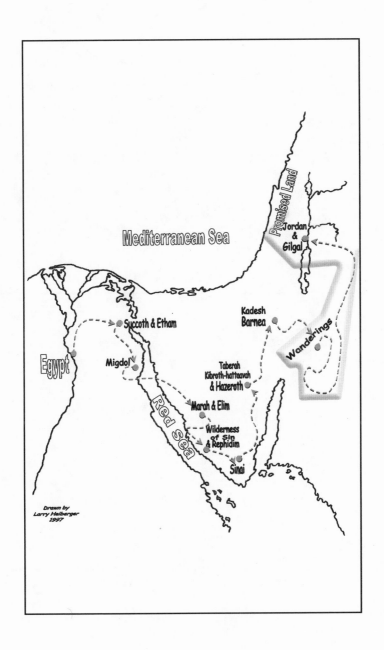

Mediterranean Sea

Promised Land

Jordan & Gilgal

Kadesh Barnea

Wanderings

Egypt

Succoth & Etham

Migdol

Red Sea

Taberah Kibroth-hattaavah & Hazeroth

Marah & Elim

Wilderness of Sin & Rephidim

Sinai

Drawn by
Larry Helberger
1997

10

GETTING RID OF MEDIOCRITY

The 40 Years of Wandering

Your carcasses shall fall in this wilderness; and all that were numbered of you, according to your whole number, from twenty years old and upward, which have murmured against me, doubtless ye shall not come into the land, concerning which I sware to make you dwell therein, save Caleb the son of Jephunneh, and Joshua the son of Nun. . . . And your children shall wander in the wilderness forty years, and bear your whoredoms, until your carcasses be wasted in the wilderness. After the number of the days in which ye searched the land, even forty days, each day for a year, shall ye bear your iniquities, even forty years, and ye shall know my breach of promise (Numbers 14:29-34).

Where Are You Going?

Some people want to get somewhere, but they haven't made up their minds where they are going. Others want to get somewhere, but they have no idea where they are headed. Then there are those who want to get somewhere, know where they are headed, and believe that with determination and direction they will get there.

The Israelites set out on a journey to leave Egypt and go into Canaan. God's plan would have allowed them to become victorious in the land of Canaan. However, they themselves were their own hindrances. No man can be a conqueror unless he first conquers himself. Getting out of Egypt is one thing, but getting Egypt out of us takes commitment. Only then can we be conquerors. I wonder how many of us have started out on 18-day journeys that took us 40 years?

The Land of Wandering

God did not intend for the children of Israel to wander 40 years. It was only an 18-day journey intended to be stretched into 18 months of pre-victory training. *This is the land of mediocrity.* People who refuse to learn have to go through the same problems over and over. Life is an endless cycle of the same thoughts, the same old scenes, and the same old surroundings. It is like an electric train under the Christmas tree that keeps circling. You never have to wonder if it's going to make a turn, make a stop to pick up a new passenger, or even slow down. At first the train is intriguing. But after a while it becomes monotonous.

You certainly don't have to look far to see mediocrity. In many cases, it's like a curse handed down from generation to generation. It simply means to "settle for less." Mediocrity means living life in a state of complacency bordered on every side by perceived limitations, financial impediments, and rude awakenings. It's the world of "Que será, será, whatever will be, will be." There are no plans for escape.

- Mediocrity is the high school graduate who is content to work the rest of his or her life on a low-income scale — with no plans for the future.

- Mediocrity woos the young couple who heads into life satisfied just to make ends meet, never stopping to think about their true potential — satisfied to remain as they are.

- Mediocrity serenades the middle-aged person who settles in at the age of 45 and feels life has been lived to its fullest — settled in and avoiding further challenges.

- Mediocrity paints life with just a tinge of hopelessness — not enough to keep you discouraged, but just enough to keep you from dreaming.

The struggle in the land of mediocrity is always there. It is a life of limitations — limited finances, limited adventures, limited vacations, limited achievements.

175

I will call this couple George and Candy. Both were born with talents in music, arts, and crafts — talents that would impress any talent scout. Both chose not to go to college. They could have afforded it, but college would delay their plans for the present. As many young couples do, they made choices based on the present, giving little or no thought to the future. Yes, they knew the future would eventually come around, but their attitude was, "Hey, we'll just cross that bridge when we get to it." They thought they had to have what they wanted immediately.

The first road sign pointing to the land of mediocrity says, "Now." This is good advice for a procrastinator, but it is not workable for the planner. George and Candy got married *now*, they had children *now*, and they bought "things" *now*. The years rolled by and they were still living in a rented home, driving old cars, and working for low wages. Because of their "now" philosophy, they *now* work longer hours than others because they make so little. Needless to say, they both work two jobs, which when combined do not match the income of one individual with a bachelor's degree. Now at the age of 50, life looks the same as it did at the age of 20 and 30.

Life in the land of mediocrity seems to go in circles. I wonder what they will do when they turn 70 and can no longer work long hours. They have no home, no retirement, no investment, and no plan.

I hope they can cross that bridge when they get to it. Their children are married and are making similar choices. Both George and Candy possessed talent and charm, but they settled for less.

"Are they happy?" you might ask. That is the goal, isn't it? If happiness is just acceptance of what life gives you, then perhaps they are. However, if happiness is fulfilling your potential, living your life to its fullest, and making a difference in the lives of others . . . well, they have never experienced these things.

Mediocrity has been called by many names. Max Lucado calls it "the thief of familiarity" (*He Still Moves Stones*, 1993). John Mason calls it "the enemy called average" (*An Enemy Called Average*, 1990). Pastor Rick Renner calls it, "the land of dream thieves" (*Dream Thieves*, 1992). It is a land of bondage . . . a place of futility . . . the land of the lost. One thing is certain: Those who dwell in the land of wandering never have a settled heart. Such people have no direction, no peace, no joy. They never taste the meal of a champion. During the Israelites' many years of wandering, they made many stops. These were significant only because of the need to bury their dead.

The Land of Winning

God made you a winner. You are at the same crossroads as Israel. The choice is this: Settle for the land of mediocrity or fight for the land of milk and honey. God prepared you to be a winner, but you must keep your sights on Canaan. The excess baggage that keeps you from running the race with swiftness must be left behind. So now what? Four things will determine whether or not you will reach your God-given potential.

1. *You must trust God and take a risk.* You have to take a risk to win. Do something bigger than yourself! That's where God is. The world is filled with overcomers — men and women who stood against the odds and won. In the early history of this century, a man decided to start a new business. He wanted to make cars. The public rejected the idea, making a joke of his "smoking machine." His first attempt failed in the first year. He tried again and ended up bankrupt. Determined to win, he tried the same business the third time. This time he did well. That man was Henry Ford.

Another company that took the risk was the Coca Cola Company, selling only 400 Cokes the first year. Today they are a worldwide company.

Another man wrote children's books. The first 23 publishers he submitted his stories to rejected him. The 24th publisher took the risk, and the first edition sold 6 million copies. That man was Dr. Seuss.

2. *You must be willing to sacrifice.* No one sacrifices anything just for today. You sacrifice only because you see the big picture. You give up something

small today for something gigantic tomorrow. John Maxwell is quoted as saying, "There is no success without sacrifice. If I succeed without sacrifice, it's because someone went before me and sacrificed."

Pastor Tommy Barnett left his church in Iowa to become the pastor of Phoenix First Assembly. The church he was pastoring averaged 5,000. The Phoenix congregation was under 1,000. Through commitment and sacrifice, he now pastors the second-largest church in the nation with a membership of over 17,000.

At the age of 65, Colonel Sanders started the Kentucky Fried Chicken franchise in his own kitchen. The product he developed is now enjoyed by millions.

3. *You must be willing to help other people.* Zig Ziglar says, "The best way to ensure to get what you want out of life is to help enough other people get what they want." We must accept the fact that we cannot make it without other people. Every talent God gives us links us to a harvest of people. Each harvest is unique. The combination of one man's gifts will open up a field of people that no one else has been designed to reach.

Many have the mistaken idea that stardom is all about pushing one's self. Exposure certainly is necessary to attain celebrity status, but what really makes a star is giving the public the product or service it demands.

Living life from a selfish perspective limits our effectiveness to others. It is only when people perceive that you are interested in helping them that you will be in demand. Give people what they want, and they will come back for more. If you take only what you want, they may never return. The idea here is not to achieve stardom but rather to make a difference in the lives of others. You may become a star and not even know it.

4. *You must begin to make long-range choices.* You can choose to live for the present, or you can make choices that will affect you throughout eternity. In his book *Seven Habits of Highly Effective People,* Stephen Covey wrote, "Begin with the end in mind." This concept does not suggest that we simply look at the bottom line or finished product, but rather look at how it will affect our lives in the end.

One of the exercises I use in counseling is to have an individual write his or her own eulogy. The discoveries are amazing. The idea is to write things you would like people to say at your funeral. I have yet to have one of my clients tell me that this is a difficult assignment. We must get out of the habit of thinking only of the present, and train ourselves to think long-range — all the way to the end if necessary.

While I was sitting in a seminar several years ago, the instructor asked us to write down 25 things we wanted to do before we died. After completing this assignment, he stated that we had just joined the ranks of only 3 percent who had ever completed that exercise.

One afternoon my phone rang. On the other end was a distraught pastor who told me how he and his wife had lost interest in the ministry. He continued by saying that she had isolated herself from him and the church, and was displaying anger in her attitudes and conversations.

After listening to him a few minutes, I asked him when he had noticed a difference in her behavior. He told me that it had started in January when he published his goals for the church that year. Upon his showing them to her, she replied, "Now where are the goals for our family this year?"

He remembered her comment only after I probed his memory. It was obvious that he had focused so much on the church that he completely omitted planning for his family. Afterward he regrouped and devised a plan for his life that included the following order: God, family, self, friends, church, and lifetime achievements.

Canaan Is Still Waiting to Be Conquered

Joshua and Caleb never stopped believing God's promises. Even though they were opposed by the multitude, they kept their eyes on Canaan. They could not get the taste of Canaan's luscious grapes out of their mouths. Their determination was greater than the challenges facing them. Their thoughts of Canaan grew in magnitude during the 40 years of wandering. You see, they had stepped into the Land of Promise. It took only one look to convince them that it would be worth the fight.

The following recitation by Howard Goodman may describe Joshua and Caleb's dreams:

I've dreamed many dreams that never came true,
I've seen them vanish at dawn;
Oh, but enough of my dreams did come true,
To keep me dreaming on.

I've prayed many prayers when no answer came,
Though I waited patiently and long;
But enough answers have come to my prayers,
To keep me praying on.

I've sown many seeds that fell by the wayside,
For the birds to feed upon;
But I've held enough golden sheaves in my hands,
To make me keep sowing on.

I've trusted many friends that have failed me,
And left me to weep alone;
But enough of my friends have been true blue,
To make me keep trusting on.

I've drunk from the cup of disappointment and
    pain,
And gone many days without a song;
But I've sipped enough nectar from the roses of
    life,
To make me want to live on.
                                        — *Author unknown*

A Lesson in Repelling

A few years ago I spoke to a group in West Vir-
ginia. A part of our group decided to go repelling.
Our guide was a fine Christian man who had experience in rock climbing. We found a challenging
150-foot rock ledge that went straight down and
over the mouth of a cave. The last 25 feet would be
a free-hanging experience. I have never been fond
of heights, but neither have I shirked a challenge.
So I was game.

The day before, we had conquered the white
waters of the mighty Galley River in a 10-man raft.
This seemed minimal in comparison . . . but there
was something else to defeat.

I watched anxiously as each person took his turn.
Some fell, others became afraid halfway down, and
one or two just walked down in a casual stroll. Finally, my turn came. I leaned over the side of the
mountain and peered into the gorge. It appeared
to be a thousand feet away. I could feel the rush of

anxiety. But I had to overcome my fears with courage. There was no way I would back out now. I had climbed the mountain and put on the gear. I was ready. The instructor began to brief me on the things I should expect. "The only way off the first lip is to lean into the rope in a squatting position and slowly back off the edge of the rocky cliff," he said. Noticing my apprehension, he drew a spiritual analogy to the experience. I will never forget his instructions:

> There is a man holding to one rope at the top and another one holding on at the bottom. These are your safety men. If you fall, they will hold you up and gently lower you off the mountain. These represent your prayer partners in life who hold you up during a crisis.
>
> The secret to getting off the mountain is to keep your feet on the rock at all times. Never take your feet off the rock. That rock beneath your feet represents Jesus. You must be able to feel it beneath you at all times. Even though you can't look down and see your next step, as long as you can feel the rock, you know that you are still on the right course.
>
> I will be the voice that talks you off the mountain. You must not look down or worry about where to step next because I will guide you with my voice. Whatever you do, don't take your eyes off me. If you look down, you

might get scared; if you look to the side, you might get confused; if you look straight ahead, you will see only two feet in front of you. Just keep your eyes on me. I represent God the Father in your life. The voice (His Word) will give the direction you need to complete this challenge.

Now you must lean into the rope. The rope is the only tangible guide you have. It never leaves your side. You may cling to it, or even hug it, but never let it go. The rope you are leaning on is already at the bottom waiting for you. That rope represents the Holy Spirit in your life. Each time you take a step while clinging or leaning to it, remember it's already there waiting. Just trust it.

I didn't quit. I steadily walked off the side of that 150-foot rock ledge. I did step into a couple of potholes, but my safety men, my guide, my rock, and my rope got me safely through. Never give up!

Getting Out of Mediocrity

Personal Evaluation

Read each of the following statements and answer **True** or **False**.

1. I am determined to be a winner. _____

2. I am willing first to conquer myself in order to conquer life. _____

3. I have been wandering in the land of mediocrity longer than I should. _____

4. I have been willing to settle for less in certain areas of my life, instead of trusting God to give me what He promised belongs to me as His child. _____

5. I haven't been patiently waiting for God's promises, but rather taking what I could get in order to have it NOW. _____

6. I have been afraid to take a risk. _____

7. I have a distinct plan for my life. _____

8. I am willing to make sacrifices today in order to be a winner tomorrow. _____

Meditate on the following questions and answer honestly.

1. Do I really know what I want in life?

2. Do I know God's will for my life?

3. Do I have long-range plans and short-term goals to help me accomplish these plans?

4. Am I willing to commit to never giving up no matter what?

Group Discussion

1. Discuss the importance of having a plan for your life.

2. Discuss the idea of "settling for less" in order to have what you want now.

3. Discuss the following statements about living in the "land of winning":

   a. You must trust God and take a risk.

   b. You must be willing to sacrifice.

   c. You must be willing to help other people.

   d. You must begin to make long-range choices.

4. Discuss the poem recited by Howard Goodman.

5. Ask a member of the group to share a personal experience or the experience of another in

which they were settling for mediocrity until God convinced them they could be a winner.

6. Discuss what it is like to live in spiritual Canaan.

7. Discuss the illustration about repelling and how it relates to our own experiences in life.

Exercise

Ask each person to sit in a chair facing the wall. (This will help them to focus on the exercise.) Give each of them a writing tablet and a pencil. The following exercise will help the members of the group to begin making long-range plans for their lives. First, ask them to write down 20 things they would like to do before they die. Next, they should write down five things they would like to accomplish this year. Last, ask them to write 10 statements they would like to have said about them at their funeral. This exercise may take a little time, but it will be very rewarding to the members of the group in determining direction for their lives.

PART III

THE PROMISED LAND AND HOW TO GET IN

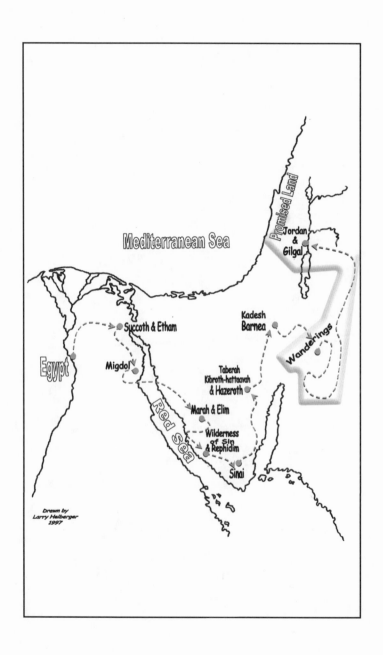

Mediterranean Sea

Promised Land

Jordan & Gilgal

Kadesh Barnea

Wanderings

Egypt

Succoth & Etham

Migdol

Taberah
Kibroth-hattaavah
& Hazeroth

Marah & Elim

Red Sea

Wilderness
of Sin
& Rephidim

Sinai

Drawn by
Larry Helberger
1997

11

THE STEP BEFORE THE FINAL STEP

Crossing the Jordan and Camping at Gilgal

And the people came up out of Jordan on the tenth day of the first month, and encamped in Gilgal, in the east border of Jericho. And those twelve stones, which they took out of Jordan, did Joshua pitch in Gilgal. And he spake unto the children of Israel, saying, When your children shall ask their fathers in time to come, saying, What mean these stones? Then ye shall let your children know, saying, Israel came over this Jordan on dry land. For the Lord your God dried up the waters of Jordan from before you, until ye were passed over, as the Lord your God did to the Red sea, which he dried up from before us, until we were gone over. . . .

At that time the Lord said unto Joshua, Make thee sharp knives, and circumcise again the children of Israel the second time. And Joshua made him sharp knives, and circumcised the children of

193

Israel at the hill of the foreskins. And this is the cause why Joshua did circumcise: All the people that came out of Egypt, that were males, even all the men of war, died in the wilderness by the way, after they came out of Egypt. Now all the people that came out were circumcised: but all the people that were born in the wilderness by the way as they came forth out of Egypt, them they had not circumcised (Joshua 4:19-23; 5:2-5).

Going Through the Jordan

The generation before had grown accustomed to the miracles of God so much that they became a part of everyday living. Manna here, quail there, a pillar of fire here, and a cloud there. Even the parting of the great Red Sea and the destruction of their foes did not strengthen their faith enough to believe God for the Promised Land. But this new generation grew up knowing only death, funerals, and wandering in the wilderness. They had heard about the miracles, but now they desperately needed to see God's hand working in their own generation.

This desire created a hunger for God and His presence. Victory is preceded by a season of hunger and thirsting. The young, inexperienced priests lined up to bear the ark of the covenant and go before the people. Little did they know they were about to enter into two new covenants with God: one of water and one of blood.

The morning came for these pilgrims to take the first step into the Promised Land (Joshua 3). Just on the other side of the Jordan River was milk and honey, but first came the river. Joshua was sure that God would part the water for them as He had for Moses and the former generation. But in the case of the Red Sea, an east wind had blown all night and parted the water. However, when the Israelites came to the Jordan, the wind was still and calm. Step-by-step the young Levites moved toward the muddy Jordan. The water streamed by in a steady flow of swirls and undercurrents, but still no parting.

Each one looked at the other as if to say, "What now?" With tenacity, the priests walked forward. They had come too far to even think about going back. They took their first step onto the muddy banks of the mighty Jordan. Still there was no move of God. With swelling faith and determination, they pursued their march into the river, bearing the ark on their shoulders. Once into the water, they noticed the currents of the river suddenly stopping. The river began to rise up like a wall. And for the first time in centuries, Jordan revealed the secrets that lay underneath her waters—smooth stones in the riverbed. The children of Israel walked across on a dry path. Just before the last tribe crossed, the leaders picked up 12 stones and carried them from the riverbed. Once on land, Joshua instructed them to build an altar (see Joshua 4:1-9). They were leaving their past behind them and moving into the promises forfeited by their forefathers. They should have been born on this land, they should have been raised on this land, they should already have been worshiping on this land. Even though they had been delayed, they had not been denied!

Before the departure from Jordan, Joshua may have addressed the pilgrims of faith by saying, "The stones we left as a memorial in the Jordan signify our hard, rough life in the wilderness. The smooth stones we extricated signify our lives we will cleanse before God this day. These stones were cleaned and purified by the washing of the water until all the rough edges were removed. So shall we be this day before the Lord of Hosts."

The Bible is explicit in noting that during the crossing of the Jordan, the river stood up "in a heap" at the city of Adam (3:15). Every person all the way back to Adam was represented by the 12 stones Joshua took from the Jordan to build an altar unto the Lord. One could compare this river crossing to baptism by water and the need to have the physical experience of going into the water as a testimonial of the inward work of grace in the heart. Their next stop was Gilgal (4:19).

Gilgal, the Place of Sanctification

"Let's call the place Gilgal," Joshua may have said. It seemed like a strange name for such a serene place. "What does the name mean?" someone asked.

Joshua answered, "It means *to roll away*" (see 5:9). God can give us His promises at will, but with each blessing comes the responsibility to share the blessing.

God's blessings are not given to store up earthly treasures. Rather they are given to increase the kingdom of God. Before God can give us His gifts, He takes us through a period of cleansing and purification so we will not be tempted to abuse His gifts. Gilgal represents a place of "rolling away," or getting rid of things that will hinder our stewardship when we come into the place of God's favor and blessings.

The Covenant of Blood

Joshua gathered the men of each tribe and assembled them at the Tabernacle. Then he began an oration by telling the story of Abraham and their forefathers. He reminded them of how God had commanded them to circumcise their race as a covenant of blood with God. The shedding of blood goes all the way back to the Garden of Eden after the fall of Adam (see Genesis 3:21).

Even though we are not actually offering literal, physical blood, the fact remains that when we come to God in repentance, He looks to the Cross where Jesus, the spotless Lamb, died and places our sins under the blood. Jesus' sacrifice paid for our sins. Spiritually speaking, at that moment of redemption, our spirit is transfused and transformed from being dead to having a living, purpose-driven existence. We have now been washed in the blood. That's why the songwriter articulated:

> What can wash away my sin?
> Nothing but the blood of Jesus;
> What can make me whole again?
> Nothing but the blood of Jesus.

> Oh! precious is the flow
> That makes me white as snow;
> No other fount I know,
> Nothing but the blood of Jesus.

As Easy as ABC

Joshua's generation, like every generation of pilgrims before, had its own stories and experiences. It is still the same today since each person must experience spiritual circumcision (see Colossians 2:11, 12). Since the death and resurrection of Christ, God has made it easy for us to be saved. It's as easy as ABC. Here is a simple formula, based on Romans 10:9:

A Admit that you have sinned.

B Believe that Christ died for your sins.

C Confess that He is Lord of your life.

Water and Blood

We have these two witnesses with us: water and blood. They are often found linked together throughout Scripture, and with good reason.

- It was water and blood that flowed from the body of Jesus as the last physical evidence of His crucifixion.

- It was water and blood that reminded Pilate that he had killed an innocent man.

- It was water and blood that were used by the high priest of the Old Testament to offer up sacrifices to God.

- It is water and blood that are part of the birthing process.

The relationship between these two elements is quite simple. They testify to the triune entity of man, reminding us that we are made in God's image—body, soul, and spirit. God is Father, Son, and Holy Spirit.

The water and blood are natural elements of the body, yet both play significant roles in helping us to understand God's spiritual plan for man. The blood cleanses our spirit by washing us in the blood of Christ; the water cleanses our soul, which is our mind, by washing us in the water of the Word.

Husbands, love your wives, just as Christ also loved the church and gave Himself for her, that He might sanctify and cleanse her with the washing of water by the word, that He might present her to Himself a glorious church, not having spot or wrinkle or any such thing, but that she should be holy and without blemish (Ephesians 5:25-27, *NKJV*).

Washing of the Word

Although the washing by the blood is an instantaneous work of God, the washing by the water of the Word is a continual process called *sanctification.* Just as we bathe our bodies each day, so should we bathe our souls with the Word of God. This bathing is the essential reason many fail to live in victory. They march into battle without having their minds conditioned for war. They declare war on their enemy, but they have a limited knowledge as to how to survive the war, once engaged in battle.

There is no victory without the daily washing by the Word. It not only makes a difference — it is the difference between victorious living and mediocre living. There is no substitute for a good bath. Cologne can't hide filth, fresh clothes can't hide stench, and a hat can't hide dirty hair. In the same way, only the Word of God can remove the filth from our minds and the stench from our attitudes. That is why the apostle Paul wrote that we are transformed by the renewing of our minds through the Word of God (Romans 12:2). That is also why he said that faith comes only through the Word of God (10:17).

The step before the final step is a time of cleansing through repentance — putting our sins under the blood and receiving more of God's thoughts than this world's thoughts. Once we apply His Word to our lives, He reveals areas of impurity. Each day God orders our steps with His Word.

The Step Before the Final Step

Personal Evaluation

Meditate on the following questions and answer honestly.

1. Can I honestly say that I am hungry and thirsty for God? (*Before answering this question, think back to the last time you were truly hungry or thirsty and remember your search to find food or drink.*)

2. Do you feel like the former Israelite generation who took God's blessings for granted?

3. Do you ever find yourself basing your faith on the stories of another generation, or are you telling your own stories about your journey with God?

4. Have you ever found yourself turning back just before the victory? Remember the faith of those young Levites who stepped into the Jordan River before the waters parted.

5. How much do you actually read the Bible?

6. How many scriptures could you quote if you did not have your Bible near you? Do you have a favorite scripture?

7. Do you know how to lead someone to Christ? Have you ever done it? When was the last time?

Group Discussion

1. Discuss the 12 stones that were taken out of the riverbed. Discuss the significance of the memorial altar built in Gilgal.

2. Ask a member of the group to give a story that was handed down from a grandparent or older Christian person which has strengthened his or her faith.

3. Discuss the importance of the cleansing process before the victory.

4. Explain what the author means by the following statement: Gilgal represents a place of "rolling away" or getting rid of things that will hinder our stewardship when we come into the place of God's favor and blessings.

5. Discuss the roles of the water and the blood in helping us to understand God's spiritual plan for man.

6. How does the washing of the Word make the difference between victorious living and mediocre living?

7. Discuss the importance of naming an altar.

8. Repeat the ABC plan of salvation until the entire group knows it by heart. Memorize Romans 10:9 while in class by repeating it several times.

9. Ask if someone in the group can describe how the washing of the Word *purges* an individual.

10. Discuss the last sentence in this chapter: "Each day God orders our steps with His Word."

Exercise

Build yourself an altar. It may only be a small one of stones or perhaps of wood. Build it with your own hands and give it a name. The Bible is filled with named altars. Each name is significant of a time when God met with His people and brought deliverance. Don't tear it down. It will be a landmark of faith for the rest of your journey with God.

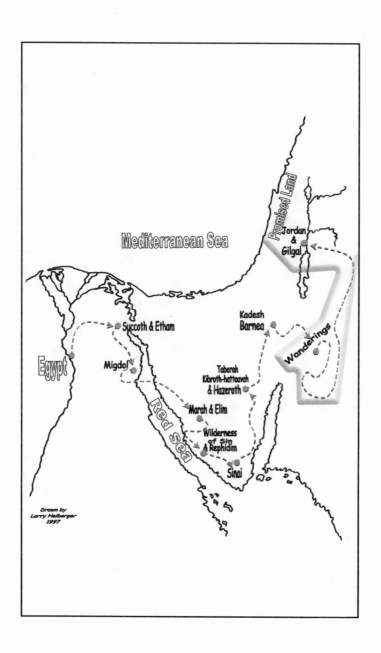

12

AT LAST—DUE SEASON

Possessing Your Promises

And let us not grow weary while doing good, for in due season we shall reap if we do not lose heart (Galatians 6:9, *NKJV*).

At Last

As the baby slips through the channel of what seems like two eternities, all the pain is forgotten. At last you have a human form to hold, tiny hands to clasp, lips to kiss, and baby's breath on your cheek. The struggling is over and the final days of discomfort diminish in the face of the miracle you hold in your arms. The only thought you can conceive in this breathtaking moment of awe is that it was worth it all.

Possessing your promises makes life worth the climb. Just to hold that reality that was once a dream brings such contentment that you drop to your knees, lift your hands, and worship the One who never fails to fulfill His promises to every pilgrim.

Canaan Land

The red-faced, battle-scared caravan finally arrived in the Land of Promise. It was everything, and more, they imagined it would be. The first thing the children did was dive into the cool mountain streams of Sidon. With the desert behind them, they began to look ahead. First, God gave them Jericho, but it was only the first of many cities and many battles. Each day the caravan pushed forward, conquering new territory and leaving a remnant of relatives behind. The tribe of Simeon was the first to settle. They immediately began building walls and altars to secure their land. Next, the tribe of Judah settled just south of Jericho. The army downsized each time a city was captured because they were home . . . in their promised land.

Eastward and northward they pushed, claiming everything in their path. The size of the army was as important as the size of their faith. The rich, fertile land had already been worked. God sometimes allows our enemies to work the land while He is storing it up for His children. The desert lessons were behind them and a new breed of God-fearing pilgrims emerged. The colors of Israel began to fly in every city; soon the land would be theirs.

"Ah, Canaan land, and what's even better . . . it is

208

our land," cried the fathers of Israel. The grape clusters were so large that two men had to carry them. The richness of the soil extended the growing season to produce twice the number of crops they had had in Egypt. There were fruit trees by the scores and an abundance of cool fresh water. The wells ran deep, the breeze remained steady, and the favor of God stilled the fear of enemy uprisings. Home at last . . . peace at last . . . joy at last! It was worth the journey.

The first evening in Canaan was a night of celebration. Tambourines, timbrels, and psalteries accompanied the dancing. The joyful praise electrified the air. The old men cried, the young men laughed, while the women talked of children growing up in new houses. Food was plenteous! Manna and quail were out, spicy herbs and fresh vegetables were in. The menu for that first feast included cooked meat, vegetables sautéed in garlic and onions, with honey, and melons and berries for dessert. It was truly the land of milk and honey. Their promise had been fulfilled. They were destined to win.

Satan Fears Your Coming Into Your Prophetic Season

The Enemy is terrified of people who have been sanctified. He sets traps and bondages to steal their

joy and hinder them from coming into their pro-
phetic season. Satan tries to rip away God's promises until all that is left is a spiritual ghost town, a
vacant house. He delights in God's children only
going through the motions.

Satan desires to sabotage your success because
you were created to win. The Potter molded you in
His image. He carefully formed you with His anvil
and hammer so you would be strong enough to win.
You were designed to be a vessel of honor, meat for
the Master's use.

You were created to walk in blessings and not
curses. You were created to walk in dignity, not in
shame. You were created to hold your head high,
to keep going and not quit. You were crafted to
soar with the eagles, not scratch in the dirt with the
chickens. You were created to "run and not be
weary, to walk and not faint" (see Isaiah 40:31). You
were not created to be stressed out, but to be strong
in battle. You were "fearfully and wonderfully
made" (Psalm 139:14) in the express image of the
God of this universe. You have His seed planted in
you. God did not call you to be hungry, lonely, isolated, and depressed. He created you to show forth
His glory . . . demonstrate His power . . . fulfill His
will!

A Promise for Every Season of Life

There is a promise and a purpose for every season

(see Ecclesiastes 3:1). Each season comes with fresh perspectives that guide us into the next season of our lives. It is our responsibility to discern the season God has us in. These seasons eventually bring us into the season of promise, which is "due season."

Due season is the season God promised for the pilgrims who do not grow weary doing the right things in the midst of adversities. However, when one area is being challenged, God can bring harvest in another area. Our temptation is to focus only on the storm, robbing us of the blessings that are coming into other areas of our lives. Therefore we need to discern our seasons and understand the purpose of each season in life.

God changes the seasons of life for the same reason He changes the seasons of the earth. This allows us to replenish our losses and rediscover dormant potentials. Every now and then, God airbrushes the earth with a blanket of snow to remind us that winter is a season of beauty as well as recuperation. Winter presents opportunities unknown in the other seasons of life. It is a time for fresh ideas. It is a time to slow down, to pause and think and thank God for what He has kept us from.

Spring is the time to plant. Summer is the season of toil and labor—hard work when you don't see the results. Fall is the season for getting ready. Some would say it is the season of harvest, but actually the harvest is a yearlong process. There is a harvest in every season of life.

Due Season

In Galatians 6:9 we read, "And let us not grow weary while doing good, for in due season we shall reap if we do not lose heart" (*NKJV*). If we endure, we will reap in "due season" — the season of promise, blessing, and fulfillment. Satan will do everything he can to keep you from due season. He will lure you to take shortcuts because he knows that in due season, whatever you put your hands to will prosper. Some people never make it to due season because they didn't come through winter, spring, summer, and fall. But for those who go all the way, we have this promise: *Do not be weary; IN DUE SEASON, you will reap if you do not faint!*

Legal documents have a space for a due date — a date when payment is due. If you are the payer, it is the day you pay up. If you are the note holder, it is the day when you are paid. There is another clause that says, "Penalty due for late payment."

God allows us to go through seasons that strengthen our faith. He not only ordained a beginning for that season, but He also ordained an end. He is not only the Alpha, He is also the Omega. God has ordained a day when the season of struggle is over. It is a divine eviction notice for the devil, which says, "Your time is up!"

212

Then I can say: "Devil, today my due season starts. I worked for it; I paid for it; I walked by faith for it; I pressed on when I wanted to quit; I prayed when I wanted to sleep; I fasted when I wanted to eat; I worked when I wanted to play. But today is payday! Today your hold is broken, your tricks are all played out, your accusations are no longer valid. The Court has just handed down the final judgment in my favor, and the Judge says you have to pay up. Pack up and get out of town. God has invoked a restraining order against you during my 'due season'! It's my time, my harvest, and my season of blessing!"

Living in Canaan

I once was a slave living in Egypt, but now I'm free and living in Canaan. Canaan land is not heaven—it is a life of victory here on earth. Once in Canaan, the desire to return to Egypt is gone. The bitterness of life was sweetened at the camp in Marah. The habit of murmuring and complaining was broken at Rephidim by divine intervention. The mountaintop experience of Sinai took care of all doubt. Stress was released at Taberah, and fear was banished at Kadesh Barnea. No more living in mediocrity; the wandering years are behind. Now we can say with Caleb, "Give me this mountain. This pilgrim is receiving the promise!"

At Last—Due Season

Personal Evaluation

Look up scriptures that you can claim to bring you into "due season." Write them down and memorize them. The following guide will help you determine areas of your life where you need to claim His promises:

1. What is your promise for health?

2. What is your promise for success?

3. What is your promise for your finances?

4. What is your promise for your marriage?

5. What is your promise for your children?

6. What is your promise for heaven?

7. What is your promise for hope?

8. What is the promise that builds your faith?

9. What is the promise that helps you feel good about yourself?

10. What is the promise that gives you peace about your salvation?

Meditate on the following questions and answer honestly.

1. Do I really believe God is who He says He is?

2. Do I really believe God can do what He says He can do?

3. Do I really believe I am who God says I am?

4. Do I really believe I can do what God says I can do?

5. Do I know the assignment God has given to me for my life?

Group Discussion

1. Discuss ways Satan tries to keep you from your due season.

2. Discuss ways of knowing that you are coming into due season.

3. Discuss with the group how many due seasons a person may have in his or her lifetime.

4. Discuss whether or not a person can have due season in one area and a season of labor in another area.

5. Discuss why we need a "getting-ready" season to precede due season.

6. Discuss the statement "Do not be weary in well doing."

7. Discuss the statement "Satan does not want you to come into your season of fulfillment."

8. Discuss seasons in life when you couldn't understand the purpose, but realized later that God used that hard season to do a good work in you.

Exercise

Have each member of the group to write one statement that sums up the assignment God has given to him or her in this life. Then have each member read the statement before the group.